Cape Horn to Starboard

Cape Horn to Starboard

JOHN KRETSCHMER

Illustrations by Molly Potter

INTERNATIONAL MARINE
PUBLISHING COMPANY
Camden, Maine

© 1986 by International Marine Publishing Company

Typeset by Journal Publications, Camden, Maine
Printed and bound by BookCrafters, Chelsea, Michigan

Published by International Marine Publishing Company
21 Elm Street, Camden, Maine 04843
(207) 236-4342

Library of Congress Cataloging-in-Publication Data

Kretschmer, John.
  Cape Horn to starboard.
    1. Kretschmer, John. 2. Voyages and travels —
1959-   . 3. Cape Horn (Chile) I. Title.
G478.K73 1986   910.4'5   85-23909
ISBN 0-87742-207-9

Contents

Preface   *vii*

1   Landlubbers   1

2   A New Epoch   22

3   Stormy Christening   38

4   An Expedition Formed   52

5   A False Start   66

6   Headwinds
        and Headaches   80

7   The War Zone   91

8   Cape Horn
        to Starboard   104

9   Rendezvous
        in Valparaiso   118

10 Becalmed   132

11 San Francisco—Finally!!   147

Preface

THE CALL OF THE HORN

"We who have seen the Horn, beating around it under square sail, or running to the east past the Isles of Ramirez, low decks awash, shrouds swiftered in, rope and canvas frozen hard, screaming fulmers soaring about our swaying masthead, we of that age of sail, old, rheumatic and salted blue, salute the Horn, our old Cape Stiff."

Captain Felix Riesenberg
Cape Horn 1939

In January 1980 you would most likely have found me cursing my engineless sailboat as she lay stranded on a sandbar somewhere in the Florida Keys. I was a bungling landlubber, a kid from the suburbs, infatuated by glossy sailing magazines and desperately wanting to learn the ways of sailors. Ah, but subtly, so subtly, the sea casts its spell. For centuries innocent boys have blindly gone off to sea and returned home with a different glint in their eyes, forever changed.

Four years later, in January 1984, I captained the first modern-day and smallest American yacht to double Captain Riesenberg's "old Cape Stiff" from east to west, against the prevailing winds and currents. I learned the hard way — I always do — that the sea is not accurately described in popular, romantic ballads. The sea is a tough taskmaster, and even today she commands respect from all those who ride on the edge of her world.

This is largely the story of a sailing voyage from New York to San Francisco by way of Cape Horn. We retraced the route of America's legendary clipper ships, the swiftest ships to ever ply the oceans. We gained a firsthand understanding and respect for those powerful ships and the men who drove them.

When we encountered vicious gales in the North Atlantic and Southern Ocean, I remembered the hearty sailors of yore. I pictured them scrambling up the ratlines in response to the mate's fierce call, "All hands on deck." Precariously perched on narrow footropes, high up in the rigging, they wrestled with stiff canvas sails. Although we controlled our small, efficient sails from the safety of the cockpit, the winds and seas that pitched our fiberglass sloop were the same.

When we encountered the utter futility of waking up to a placid ocean day after day, week after week, I understood why some zealous captains were driven to madness and had to be locked in their quarters. When my grandfather, my special friend, lay dying on a hospital bed, I wanted desperately to be near him; but I was trapped in a Pacific Ocean prison cell, so vast, yet so confining.

This book is not just a collection of day-to-day log entries to our voyage. This is the story of many different sailors: my mother, my lover, and my friends among them. They are sailors of different ages and from different stations in life, but we all were serving an apprenticeship to the sea.

I have heard many reasons why sailors go to sea. Some are searching, some are striving, and some are running. I know one thing is certain; we have all been serenaded by the sea's call. For me it was the distinct call of Cape Horn, and, as John Masefield put it:

*"It's a wild call and a clear call
that may not be denied."*

Special thanks to my crew: Molly Potter, Ty Techera, Bill Oswald. Thanks to Edd Kalehoff and John Evans in New York. Thanks to Scott Palmer in St. Thomas. Thanks to Alexander Levi and Bennit in Rio. Thanks to Mario Sepulveda in Valparaiso. Thanks to Jim Nugent in San Francisco. Thanks to the Stroh Brewery Company of Detroit and all those involved with *Signature*. Thanks to Dan Belknap of Anthony M. Franco Inc. Thanks to Maureen Kretschmer, Liz Kretschmer, and Terri Gerlach for typing the manuscript. Thanks to Philip W. Mason for his support and Margaret Holland for her editing. Special thanks to all those who helped us prepare for the voyage and along the way.

1

Landlubbers

JOHN, I'M REVOKING YOUR scholarship. I'm sorry son, but you have missed too many practices and meetings, and the Dean has informed me that you're scholastically ineligible again this term. Young man, you have a disconcerting lack of discipline, even for a pole-vaulter! I'm out of patience. It's time for you to grow up. Don't forget to return your uniform and clean out your locker."

I staggered out of the coach's office in a daze and wandered off toward my dormitory. My head was reeling. What would I do next? Michigan State was my fourth university in two years; clearly it was time to change tacks.

I detoured to the library and climbed the back stairs to the fifth floor, the silent region of the library known as "the stacks." I should have called home, but I dreaded talking to my mother; she would be so disappointed. Instead, I sat at a secluded carrel and despondently paged through an out-of-date issue of *National Geographic*.

As I considered my future options and mindlessly flipped the pages, a photograph of a rusty fishing trawler caught my eye. Halfheartedly, I started to read the accompanying text. The author's powerful prose quickly commanded my full attention and fueled my imagination. It said something like this: "Modern-day adventurers cut from the Hemingway mold, the hearty fishermen routinely brave the stormy waters of the Gulf of Alaska in search of salmon and profits — profits that parallel the wild gold rush days. Alaska is still America's last frontier."

I was intrigued and skipped my next class to read the article again. "The last frontier," I said aloud, "that has the right ring to it. The last frontier. Yes, of course, the last frontier, the last goddamn frontier. That's where I belong."

I came to life and raced down the stairs, leaping a flight at a time. Dashing across campus, I was oblivious to my fellow students. In my mind's eye I was already somewhere on the Gulf of Alaska, battling wind and wave and hauling in netloads of salmon. "I'll show everybody," I blurted out. "I swear I will. I'll burst out of this academic cocoon once and for all." I made up my mind to go to Alaska and not return until I amassed a fortune and a bundle of sea stories.

That evening, when I called my mom, I tried a diplomatic approach to explain my sudden change of plans. Mom saw through my ruse and interrupted me. "Johnny, did you get kicked off the team again?" How did she know? "Well Mom, um . . . sort of, I guess . . . I mean . . . well, yes." She sighed. She didn't rant and rave, but I knew she was keenly disappointed. Although I felt miserable, I mustered enough enthusiasm to explain my desire to seek fame and fortune in Alaska. I expected her to vehemently oppose my idea, but, to my surprise, she didn't. After thinking it over for a minute, she did not try to dissuade me; in fact, she agreed with me and thought that Alaska might be just the place for me.

My mother's blessing was the only impetus I needed to put my plan into action. I officially withdrew from school the next day and bade farewell to my chums. Already my friends seemed provincial; they were anchored in East Lansing, while I was destined for the last frontier. I hastily loaded up my car and set off for Hillsdale, Michigan, 50 miles to the south, where my girlfriend, Molly, attended the local college.

Molly wasn't convinced that I was cut out for the last frontier, and our last night together was miserable. She just didn't understand my sudden, almost fanatical fascination with Alaska. "You've never been near the place," she complained, "yet you talk about it reverently." I tried to cheer her up in the morning by assuring her that I'd only be gone a couple of months. "I'll be back before the end of the summer, baby, and I'll have enough money to buy a sailboat, and then we'll sail around the world. Besides, there is nothing to worry about — I've read that there are 10 males to every female up there." Molly looked at me skeptically while tears streamed down her face.

Driving home on the interstate, I set the cruise control on 80. Buoyed with reckless, innocent optimism, I felt as though I'd cast shackles off my ankles. No more track coaches to pester me; no more papers to write; no more exams; and no more didactic professors explaining the world to me. For the first time in my life I was going to see the world for myself.

At home in suburban Detroit, I gathered up all the items needed to conquer the last frontier. Although I'd only considered the trip a week before, it had assumed great urgency, as though some greedy fishermen might catch all the fish before I got there. However, as Mom and I drove to the train station across the Canadian border in Windsor, the nagging second thoughts that I had suppressed during the euphoria of planning the trip began to creep out of the back chambers of my mind.

Standing in the ticket line with my overloaded backpack tilting me forward, I realized that there was literally no backing out this time. As I inched closer to the ticket window, I could feel my confidence ebbing. I no longer saw myself as an intrepid explorer or as a modern-day forty-niner. Instead, I saw myself as a lazy, nineteen-year-old kid from the suburbs who didn't even know how to bait a hook with a worm! "How will I manage on a commercial rig?"

"Where to?" the clerk asked.

"Um," I glanced at my mom. She was smiling; I think she was actually proud of me. "Prince Rupert," I answered softly.

"Prince Rupert," the clerk repeated. "Wow, that's a mighty long way, son — four days by train."

I boarded the Canadian-Pacific train and rode the rails westward. We rambled through Superior's north woods, across the plains of Saskatchewan, over the Rockies, and finally beyond the Coast Mountains. From Prince Rupert, British Columbia, an isolated fishing village on the shores of the Pacific, I hopped a ferryboat and sailed north for Juneau.

Day after day, for six frustrating weeks, I pounded the docks at Juneau Harbor and the Douglas Boat Basin. The docks were jammed with kids my age who had migrated north from California and the Pacific Northwest, lured by the mystique of the last frontier. I think we had all read the same article, but unfortunately it neglected to mention that Alaska's fishing industry was suffering the same recession that plagued the rest of the country. Crew jobs were scarce, and the alternative — working in a salmon canning factory — wasn't up to my romantic standards.

I was disillusioned not only with the fishing industry, but with the

3

last frontier in general. I did not expect it to be overcrowded, and to have amenities like Holiday Inns and Kentucky Fried Chickens. In desperation, I took a job as a tour-bus driver. I chauffeured tourists around town, reciting history and local lore like a native — hell, I'd only been there six weeks. By the end of July I'd had enough of the last frontier; I could not point out one more totem pole. I scraped enough money together to buy a plane ticket home to Michigan.

In the eyes of many, my brief foray to the last frontier appeared to have been an unmitigated failure, just another one of my cockeyed schemes gone astray. But I knew otherwise. Although I did not reap either fame or fortune, I did succeed in breaking out of the suffocating pattern offered by our all-too-secure society. The seeds of wild wanderlust were firmly planted in my mind, and they have flourished ever since.

Detroit seemed stifling, and I was depressed. The summer was racing by and my future was uncertain. Although I had made tentative plans to go back to school in the fall, I really longed to keep traveling and see the world.

One night in mid-August, I picked my mom up at her office, and we went out to dinner. My mom is legendary for her spontaneity, and as we sat sipping a glass of wine she threw an interesting proposition my way. "Johnny, do you really want to go back to school? Let's face it, honey, you've already blown it four times. I know that you are not that stupid — maybe you're not cut out for college."

I confessed that I wasn't enthusiastic about returning to school, but it seemed like the only sensible thing to do.

"The sensible thing is not always the best thing," Mom informed me, using curious logic. "Why don't I just give you the money I am going to spend on your tuition next semester?"

"Are you serious, Mom?"

"I sure am, but there is one stipulation."

"Ah ha," I thought to myself. I knew there had to be a catch.

"You love sailing, don't you, honey? You are always reading those silly sailing magazines." Mom is a born con artist and she was skillfully setting me up.

"Of course I do, Mom. You know that." When I was younger our family had owned a 28-foot sloop, and we had daysailed on Lake St. Clair and Lake Huron. I'd also sailed dinghies on Higgins Lake in northern Michigan.

"What's the point, Mom?"

"My point is this. You must use the money I give you, plus money you can raise by selling your car and stocks, to buy yourself a little cruising sailboat. You have talked about sailing off into the sunset for years. Now, my son, I'm going to give you the opportunity.''

I was shocked, and started sputtering before Mom interrupted me again. ''I think you had the right idea with your ill-fated trip to Alaska. Traveling teaches you things you'll never learn in school — especially you, because you can't learn if you don't attend class. Besides, Johnny, looking back I wish I'd roamed a bit farther before I got married and started having all you crazy kids. But those were different times — we had a world to save, or at least we thought we did. There wasn't time to be frivolous. I think caring for the boat and having to support yourself with it will be the strong dose of responsibility you need.'' Then she smiled at me and said, ''If you work hard for the rest of the summer and fall, I'll bet you can sail south before the snow. There, Johnny, my lecture is finished. Now, what do you say?''

''Oh, Ma, I can't believe it. That's the best idea I've ever heard! I promise I'll make the most of this — I won't screw up again — I promise. Whew boy!'' I wrapped my mother in a bear hug and squeezed until she gasped.

Mom contributed two semesters' tuition, or about $4,000. I promptly sold my car and the stocks I'd accumulated with social security payments since the death of my father three years before. I also sold my 10-speed bike, stereo, and many of the other dire necessities of suburban life. I raised the staggering sum of $8,400, which only seemed staggering until I started shopping around for a boat.

Every day I scoured the classified ads in the *Detroit News.* On weekends Molly and I (our romance patched up and sizzling again) drove to Mt. Clemens and rode along the shore of Lake St. Clair. We looked at many boats, ranging from an unsightly but roomy 22-footer to a twenty-year-old Pearson Coaster. Most of the boats we inspected were too small to contemplate for serious cruising and living aboard, and those that were not were usually priced out of my league. Also, I wasn't exactly sure what kind of boat I wanted. I had read many books filled with advice. I had learned about different keel configurations. I had worked various formulas calculating different ratios, and had studied different rigs. Yet the more I read, the more confused I became. It was my great fortune to stumble accidentally upon the *Lobster Mobster.*

I had borrowed my sister's car and driven down to the lake one afternoon during the week. I spotted a lonely sailboat in a rickety cradle in a boatyard well up the Clinton River. The yard was locked up, but I scaled the barbed-wire fence and quietly crept over to the boat. She was beautiful. She had a lot of sheer and salty, seaworthy lines. I was delighted to see a "For Sale" sign taped to the bow pulpit. The sign noted that the *Lobster Mobster* ("What an awful name," I mumbled) was a 1966 Bristol 27 sloop, designed by Carl Alberg and built of fiberglass. Then in bold letters it emphasized, **MUST SELL.**

I had a feeling that at last I'd found my dream boat, and I excitedly climbed aboard. The boat was filthy on deck and had obviously been neglected for a long time. Still, she struck me as being very sturdy. I pushed open the creaky hatch and brushed away cobwebs. Her cozy, traditional interior was perfect for the Spartan lifestyle I envisioned. I jotted down the phone number and hurried home.

That evening when I called the owner I could barely conceal my anticipation. He gave me a description of the boat's equipment. She had five sails, including a spinnaker; a single-burner alcohol stove; a self-contained porta-potty for a head; and a very minimal amount of other gear. Then I asked him what he was asking for her. He paused for a moment, then replied, "I need to clear at least 10 grand."

I winced — that was more than I had to spend. I put my hand over the phone and whispered the price to my mom. She said, "Johnny, do you really like the boat?"

"Yes, Mom, I really want it, but that's a lot of money."

"Make a low-ball offer, honey. You can always negotiate."

I swallowed hard and took a deep breath. "Well, sir, you know she needs a lot of work. I'll offer $8,500." Then, trying to sound like a big wheel, I threw in, "Cash."

The owner countered by lowering his price to $9,000. That was a rock-bottom figure he pleaded, and he was a good salesman because I promptly accepted his counteroffer. The owner said he'd clean up the boat and launch her before the weekend, so I could sail her and finalize the deal.

I secured a loan for the balance from my sister, Liz, who, although just sixteen years old, was already a shrewd financier, and Molly and I tried out the boat on Saturday. *Lobster Mobster* (the owner managed a fish market, hence the name) sailed like the wind, dancing across the lake on a broad reach. Even a sputtering outboard engine and a few patched-up sails could not dim my enthusiasm, and I went ahead and bought her. The change in my personality was marked as I gained confidence sailing my little sloop. The up-and-down life of John Kretschmer reached new heights. I finally had the vehicle to fulfill my dreams. I was my own man; I was captain of my soul, master of my fate, and all that sort of stuff. The last frontier was behind me, but the new, watery frontier lay ahead. If I had known what a stormy apprenticeship awaited me, I would never have left Lake St. Clair.

For several summers I had operated a rather casual window-washing business. I worked just hard enough to make money for dates and keep Mom off my back. However, as the summer of 1979 reached the dog days, I started to work furiously. I needed money, a lot of money. I had to purchase equipment for the boat and salt a stash away for my passage south to Florida. I was shocked at how nonchalantly *Jeanne* (I renamed the boat in honor of my mother) gobbled up my hard-earned funds.

In late August Molly and I began to work together. Molly's disciplined work ethic was just what the Shiny Window Co. needed. We must have washed the windows of every house in the neighborhood. Our relationship was wonderfully unique. By day we were chums and business partners, and by night we were lovers.

Most of our nights were spent sailing *Jeanne* on Lake St. Clair. Molly was a natural helmsman and loved sailing. *Jeanne*'s cozy cabin afforded us the privacy we craved. It was maddening to pack up and leave the boat every night. We constantly talked about sailing away together, but the burden of parental expectations proved to be a temporary roadblock to our dreamy plans. In September Molly returned to college.

As autumn descended upon the Midwest, I grew despondent. I missed Molly. She'd transferred to Florida State University in Tallahassee to bridge the distance between us when, and if, I ever sailed south. However, my business had slowed down, and I was still short of money. Unless I left soon for the passage across the Great Lakes and down the Intracoastal Waterway, I faced the prospect of another dreary Michigan winter.

One afternoon while I was driving to the boat, I noticed a sailboat riding piggyback on a flatbed truck. A light clicked on in my brain, and I realized I had an alternative to the Intracoastal Waterway; I could ship *Jeanne* on I-75 instead.

After a few inquiry calls I realized I had just enough money to ship *Jeanne* by truck. I made all the arrangements with a California-based company. Although I thought my instructions were very explicit, nothing went according to plan.

The driver mistakenly picked up *Jeanne* three days early, just after I'd taken most of her gear home for a scrubbing. Then he dropped her off at the wrong boatyard in Miami. When I arrived in Miami, *Jeanne* was inaccessible to me because the yard was locked up tight for the four-day Thanksgiving holiday. I spent the long weekend in a fleabag in the dilapidated section of Miami Beach.

I eventually launched *Jeanne* on the Miami River and survived a harrowing passage downstream. The outboard stalled several times, and more than once I narrowly avoided smashing into a slow-raising bridge.

Yet once I was clear of the river, I forgot all the previous hardships. *Jeanne* and I were finally in the land of sunshine and reaching across Biscayne Bay. When I dropped the hook behind Dinner Key off Coconut Grove, I had three immediate objectives: to convince Molly to join me, to prepare *Jeanne* for ocean sailing, and somehow to get some money together.

Although Molly and I had been dating just two years, we were in love. Our idyllic summer together had only heightened the pain of separation. Our romance had already endured my wayward journey to Alaska and other obstacles that would have snuffed out a less passionate relationship. We both knew that we would never be satisfied with occasional weekend visits. At twenty years old, love is urgent.

I called Molly from a public phone on the quayside in early December, arguing persuasively that she should interrupt her studies and join me, at least temporarily. Molly had a tough decision to make. She was an honor student and a star on the cross-country team; furthermore, if she dropped out of school her parents would be furious. But I was relentless. I pleaded and cajoled and pointed out that I was offering her the opportunity of a lifetime. Our worldly travels, I promised her, would be far more educational than a sterile classroom. Finally, maybe just to get me off the phone, Molly agreed to ship aboard *Jeanne* at the end of the semester. Ironically, in our first six months of cruising, our worldly travels took us all the way from Miami to the Dry Tortugas, a distance of about 200 miles. They were, however, a very educational 200 miles.

I desperately wanted to have *Jeanne* in shipshape condition before Molly arrived, and I hastily tackled the many projects on my long list of repairs. As the consummate mechanical hack, at times I wondered if I was causing more damage than I was correcting. I was thankful that *Jeanne* was laid up like a Sherman tank, otherwise she would never have survived my well-intentioned assaults.

For example, *Jeanne*'s long boom was tended by an awkward, transom-mounted mainsheet, and it was difficult to control the mainsail when running before the wind. Knowing there had to be a better arrangement, I decided to install a mainsheet traveler and a two-part block and tackle.

I purchased a couple of pieces of mahogany for the traveler base and all the necessary fittings. Skillfully, I planed and sanded the wood. Then I mounted an aluminum track on the mahogany and bolted the assembly across the cockpit. I was almost bursting with pride; for once I hadn't butchered a project — it looked professional. To complete the job I had only to hang the boom fitting and reeve the mainsheet. Unfortunately, mounting the final fitting required that I drill two matching holes through each side of the boom. Carefully, I made my measurements, then I confidently drilled away. Thirteen holes later, *Jeanne* looked as though she'd been riddled by terrorists, and I still couldn't jam the damn fitting through the misaligned holes! I looked at the mutilated boom and wanted to cry, but there was no one to turn to for help. In desperation I drilled another hole with my rusty hand drill, and with a lot of gentle persuasion I finally conned the fitting home.

Shipboard morale improved drastically when Molly moved aboard just before Christmas. Although we were very inexperienced sailors, our long-term goal was to sail clear around the world. Prudently, we realized we were not prepared for a circumnavigation, and we decided to make the Florida Keys our training area. But before we could even start training, we needed some money.

Molly worked in a fancy French bakery while I worked on the boat. At night we paged through the small-craft chart of the Keys, plotting an extensive cruise. Even after we had enough money to set sail, however, we still had one particularly nasty chore to take care of before we could sail with clear consciences — we had to confront Molly's parents.

Molly had decided to forego her education without first consulting her folks. Understandably, they were shocked and angered when she called from Miami and informed them that she was not returning to school. She tried the same lines I had used on her, but they didn't work. I'm not sure what she was expecting them to say, but when she hung up the phone she was devastated. "Of course they're upset, Molly," I said, trying to comfort her. "You dropped a bombshell on them. After the initial shock passes, they'll get over it." Molly was crying. She tried to call her parents back but they refused her collect call. I realized that we had to do something, or Molly would be miserable aboard *Jeanne*. I suggested that we return to Michigan and confront her parents together.

On the flight north Molly was a nervous wreck. I ached for her and tried to cheer her up. I told her that I would turn on the charm and convince her parents that the merits of our scheme far outweighed the risks. I even boasted that when I was through with them they would applaud our courage at choosing the road less traveled.

On the appointed evening, I arrived at Molly's house, but she intercepted me at the back door. Her voice was shaky as she whispered, "John, it's never going to work." Then she led me before the firing squad in the family room. We had barely settled ourselves on the couch before the barrage began. I suspected that her folks didn't like me and I was right; they accused me of corrupting Molly.

"I absolutely forbid you from taking my daughter on that crazy boat of yours ever again!" roared Molly's father, practically foaming at the mouth. "Who in the hell do you think you are?" It was not a question meant to be answered. "I'll tell you who you are. Nobody, that's who. You're a spoiled brat. Just because your mom bought you a goddamned boat doesn't make you an expert. What experience do you have? The ocean is no place for foolhardy amateurs. What you need is a job and a kick in the pants!"

I couldn't get a word in before Molly's mom took up the volley. "Oh my, for God's sake, if you really loved her and truly respected her, you would at least let her finish her education."

"Don't worry," Molly's father hollered. "Molly is going back to school, and that's final."

So much for charm. There obviously wasn't a lot of room for compromise. My feeble protests that Molly was old enough to make her own decisions were overwhelmed by stern warnings. "Go ahead and waste your life, son, but you won't waste Molly's." Truthfully, I found myself sympathizing with them. I was stealing their baby away from them, and Mr. Potter was right — what experience did I have?

However, when he started to ridicule my "useless trip to Alaska" as an example of my immaturity, I lost my temper and stormed out of the house. I didn't have to put up with that. Strangely, Alaska was still sacred to me.

Molly dashed after me. "Don't worry, baby," she sobbed, "I'm still coming. Oh, Johnny, I love you."

But as I squealed out of the driveway, I didn't know if I'd ever see her again.

Early the next morning Molly knocked at our door. With her old-fashioned suitcase in hand, she looked like Tatum O'Neal straight out of *Paper Moon*. She had made her decision — she was casting her fate to the wind.

In what was to become a chronic condition, we were short of funds when we returned to Miami. The airline fares had zapped most of our resources and provisions claimed the rest. Still, on January 7, 1980, with a new year and decade to inspire us, we set sail for Elliott Key, 20 miles to the south.

The Keys are overcrowded with people, mobile homes, condominiums, and shoals. Outlandishly, I've heard the Keys compared with the Bahamian Out Islands and Virgin Islands. The truth is, the Keys are flat and beachless, and protected anchorages are scarce. However, what the Keys lack geographically, I must admit they make a valiant effort to make up for with character.

The residents are a zany combination of outdated buccaneers, early

American rednecks, zealous real-estate developers, wild west shrimpers, and chic, San Francisco–style gays. We visited most of the major islands, and we have fond memories of the overrated archipelago of cementlike marl spits south of the mainland. The Keys taught us saltwater sailing, tolerated our many mistakes, and spawned dreams of far-off places.

The wind was light, and I tried to convince the old Mercury outboard to come to life as we drifted slowly south. I pulled and primed and kicked and cursed, but the engine would not ignite. I was sure that it had finally called it a career, but I went ahead and removed the plastic covering and examined the guts anyway. I might just as well have been staring at the circuitry of a nuclear reactor. Primarily to appease Molly, I tinkered with a few levers and springs, replaced the covering, and hopefully pulled the starter cord. Nothing, not even a whimper.

Cruising without an engine is challenging, but it's probably the best way to learn to sail. Although I had daysailed for years on the Great Lakes, I was encountering salt water, coral reefs, and nasty things such as tidal currents for the first time. We literally bounced our way south from Elliott Key through shallow Florida Bay. Whenever *Jeanne* strayed too far off course and we felt the familiar thud as the keel hit bottom, I would leap over the side and quickly push her free. Groundings were not serious, but they were aggravating. At Key Largo we decided to cross over to the deeper, Atlantic side of the Keys.

Angelfish Creek slices through the mangroves north of Key Largo and is the only deepwater passage before Matecumbe Key. Of course, deep water in the Keys means a controlling depth of 4 feet. I am probably the only sailor in the world who has been around Cape Horn but still trembles at the thought of sailing through Angelfish Creek.

On January 29, 1980, which ironically is the same day we would approach Cape Horn four years later, we made our first attempt at Angelfish. The southeast wind was on our nose, and the swift tidal stream was foul. All morning we tacked back and forth, trying to make headway in the narrow passage. At noon we had netted about 20 yards to the good, and decided to anchor and wait for a favorable wind and current.

I spent the rest of the afternoon studying a new phenomenon called tides while Molly painted the forward cabin. When she triumphantly announced she was finished, I went forward to take a look. I was stunned. She had decorated the forepeak with a dizzying array of brown and yellow geometric stripes. It looked like a huge beehive, and I was nearly seasick just staring at it. "It's unique," I said, without much enthusiasm. Fortunately, I talked her out of painting the rest of the interior.

The wind shifted to the southwest in the morning, and we glided through Angelfish Creek at slack water. I felt like Ponce de Leon when we cleared the last channel marker in the Atlantic and tacked south. A whole chain of tropical islands stretched out before us. Although it seems to the sailor that the eastern edge of the Keys is bordered by the boundless Atlantic, you're actually sailing in Hawk Channel. A string of reefs about 5 miles offshore parallels the Keys. The reefs are well marked and serve to break up the seas without hindering the fresh, easterly tradewinds. Hawk Channel is usually a great place to sail, but Molly and I were not prepared for the gusty, 25-knot headwinds we encountered.

Jeanne pitched about in the choppy seas, and we quickly realized that we could not leave pots and pans and other assorted items lying around the cabin. When Molly's paint can spilled its sickly brown contents all over the teak sole, I decided it was time to reef. I let go the halyard and struggled with the flapping mainsail. The roller-reefing boom jammed and I couldn't raise or lower the sail. Humiliated, I decided to retreat to Angelfish Creek and seek shelter from the strong winds.

Molly noticed a small tributary sprouting to the north, halfway through the creek. Skillfully, she luffed the jib and I dropped the anchor; but the bottom was rocky, and the Danforth just skipped along while the current swept *Jeanne* into the mangrove bushes along the bank.

Some people fear the ocean, some fear heights, and some fear dentists. I hate swamps; they terrify me. Angelfish Creek looks like a part of the Amazon Basin, and it does not require much imagination to envision alligators, water moccasins, and other slimy creatures lurking in the water. After a spate of cursing, mostly directed toward the useless outboard engine perched on the transom, I reluctantly eased myself into the water and pushed *Jeanne* free. Several times I swam to the middle of the channel and reset the anchor, but it just wouldn't bite.

When I refused to stay in the water a moment longer, Molly came up with a clever idea. We launched the dinghy and I rowed to the opposite bank. I secured a line around a stout mangrove bush and Molly took up the slack on the bow. *Jeanne* came to rest peacefully in the middle of the tributary.

I lashed the dinghy alongside and climbed back aboard. We congratulated each other; we had dealt with adversity and had won, or at least broken even. I told Molly that we really had the mettle to make the cruising life work, and we spent the rest of the afternoon paging through the world atlas. I told her that one day I'd like to sail around Cape Horn, but when I showed her where it was on the map, she just laughed. It seemed a world away.

A 21-year-old skipper.

No sooner had we gone below and snuggled into the beehive than I noticed a mangrove branch poking through the forward hatch. The tide had changed, as tides do, and I had failed to realize that the current would change with it. *Jeanne* was back in the mangroves. I scrambled out of bed and jumped into the dinghy. It was raining, and as I was naked and cold I worked quickly. I rowed another line to the opposite bank and secured it to a stump. Then, for good measure, I rowed a third line farther upstream. *Jeanne* looked like a huge spider spinning a web when Molly pulled the lines taut, but we felt she was finally secure.

In the middle of the night the tide changed once again, but *Jeanne* was unable to swing freely. Instead, one of her mangrove tethers snagged under the keel, and as the current picked up she heeled over 45 degrees. There was nothing we could do short of cutting one of the lines, which would have sent us careening back into the mangroves, so we spent the rest of the night pretending we were in a gale, eagerly awaiting dawn.

At first light we freed *Jeanne* from the tangled mess of lines and sailed into calm Hawk Channel, vowing never to return to Angelfish Creek. Four days later we arrived in Marathon on Vaca Key. We were flat broke. In fact, we had subsisted on a meager diet of popcorn and French salad dressing for the previous couple of days. We anchored in Boot Key Harbor, a refuge for down-on-their-luck cruisers, and rowed ashore. I called my mom in Michigan and asked her to wire us money so that we could survive until one of us found a job.

I was hired by the Marathon Car Wash and came to learn the true meaning of the late Jim Croce's memorable song, "Working at the Car Wash Blues":

"I've got those steadily depressing, low-down mind messing, working at the car wash blues."

For three weeks I endured a miserable routine for the less-than-minimum, starvation wage of $2.75 an hour. On a typical morning I was up and about at 6:30 A.M. After a quick bowl of cereal and powdered milk, Molly and I rowed the three-quarters of a mile to shore. I'd kiss Molly goodbye and start the 4-mile trek to the car wash. I couldn't even thumb a ride, because hitchhikers are thrown in jail in the Keys. Conscientious as ever, I'd invested a precious $7 in a pair of Jack Percel sneakers to be properly prepared for the job. Unfortunately, the stiff Jack Percels cut my feet to ribbons, but I had to hobble right along because the car wash opened at 7:30 sharp.

Once at the car wash, I soloed on the exit side. Believe me, that sounds more glamorous than it was. All day long, as cars came through the wash, I wiped them dry, cleaned the windows inside and out, dumped the ashtrays, polished the mirrors, and replaced the mats. The car wash did a booming business, and I worked like a maniac. At 5:30 P.M., I limped 4 miles back to the dock with my soaked Jack Percels, feeling as though they weighed 50 pounds each. Molly rowed me out to the boat and I collapsed into bed. Ah, the glamorous cruising life.

As if being broke and harbor-bound and having a severe case of the car-wash blues were not enough, Molly informed me one day after work that she thought she was pregnant. For a week we nervously awaited the results of her pregnancy test. When things turned up negative, we were ecstatic. We bought a couple of bottles of cheap wine and proceeded to throw three sheets to the wind. Then we very carefully continued our celebration in the beehive.

I happily quit the car wash in mid-February, just a few days before Mom and my sister, Liz, flew down for a visit. We spent a delightful week daysailing all around the middle Keys. Molly and I even accepted Mom's generous offer of a room at the Holiday Inn and enjoyed our first hot shower in months.

To my surprise, Mom thoroughly enjoyed each day's sail aboard *Jeanne*. She whooped with joy as we buried the lee rail on a wild, windward slug south to Duck Key. After we secured the boat at the Indies Isle

Marina, Molly and Liz hurried off to explore the island while Mom and I sipped a beer at the hotel bar. She confided in me that she was weary of her routines up north, and with Lizzy away at college the big house was lonely. I suggested she take a month off and sail with us. Although she declined the offer, claiming that *Jeanne* was too small for three people and that she would be intruding in our lives, I could tell by the look in her eyes that my idea had hit home. As she gazed at the white horses charging down Hawk Channel, the first seeds of an alternate lifestyle were planted in her mind. They would only need a few more months of dreary Michigan weather, the day-to-day drudgery of business, and a ripening wanderlust to blossom into a full-blown scheme for escape.

Mom and Liz returned to the real world, and Molly and I continued our voyage. On March 1, 1980, we set sail for Key West. We beat down Middle Sister Creek, a shortcut to the ocean, but as the narrow creek emptied into the open sea I made a terrible mistake that nearly set *Jeanne* on the rocks.

The creek was well sheltered, and I underestimated the strength of the wind as we entered the marked channel leading to deep water. I also overestimated the depth of the water — a grave mistake in the Keys. Molly was at the helm, and I told her to head into the wind as I scurried forward to shorten the headsail. Just as I let the halyard run, we grounded on a sandbar at the edge of the channel.

"Come about now!" I screamed.

"I can't, the tiller's hard over. We're stuck!" Molly yelled back.

Foolishly, I raised the genoa back up, hoping we might be able to jibe over and free the boat. But a sudden gust filled the half-hoisted sail and pushed *Jeanne* over the sandbar into very shallow water. We were hard aground just 200 yards off a rocky lee shore, with a stiff onshore wind blowing!

We both plunged into the water and tried to push *Jeanne* free, but we were losing the fight. *Jeanne* was pounding heavily and slowly drifting toward the rocks. A passing fisherman noticed us struggling in the water and offered to help. I warned him not to come too close — the water shoaled abruptly. Instead, I swam our longest and strongest line out to his boat. He secured the line to a stern cleat and revved up both engines on his small runabout. He pulled one way and then the other, but *Jeanne* remained fast. I kept my shoulder to the hull and pushed with all my heart. Molly frantically emptied our heaviest gear into the dinghy. Just when we were all about to admit defeat, *Jeanne* surged forward. The fisherman used her momentum to dredge a channel through the sand as Molly and I excitedly swam after her.

Amazingly, *Jeanne*'s heavily laid up hull was only superficially scratched and structurally undamaged. We'd been lucky, plain and simple. The fisherman refused to take anything for his services — it was a good thing, too, because we had little to offer. We thanked him again and again, but he just smiled and waved his hand and then zoomed away. As corny as it may sound, there is still a camaraderie among those who ply the sea, and there is but one tenet: HELP THOSE IN DISTRESS. We were too frazzled after our near disaster to press on. We returned to Boot Key Harbor the safe way, through the main channel.

We restored our confidence with a six-pack of Miller, and in the morning we set off again. March in the Keys is lovely — the spring weather settles in and the tradewinds blow steadily. Our passage to Key West was pleasant enough until we were rudely interrupted by the U.S. Coast Guard.

We were just a few miles southeast of Key West, minding our own business, when a Coast Guard cutter steamed toward us. The cutter hardly slowed down before it came alongside and whacked into *Jeanne* amidships. Two crewmembers stood by with their rifles trained at my head while two others jumped aboard, mumbling something about "permission" in midair. Molly scrambled for her clothes, because she'd been enhancing her all-over tan. The Coast Guardsmen recklessly rummaged through the cabin, looking in all the nooks and crannies. When they were satisfied that we were not smuggling drugs, they hopped back on their boat and roared away. I was furious. "That was an act of piracy! The bastards."

When we arrived in Key West later that day, we found out what the fuss was about. A smuggler, obviously on the verge of being apprehended, had unloaded his marijuana by the bale. Amazingly, the bales of dope had drifted right into Key West Harbor. The residents, delirious with joy, had rushed down to Mallory Square to reap the gift from the god of the sea.

We anchored off Christmas Tree Island, opposite old Key West, and savored the historic city's unique charms. This time it was Molly's turn to work, and she was hired as a clerk in a head shop. She sold scales and various paraphernalia to marijuana and cocaine dealers. It was a low-key job because the manager spent most of the day in the back room, stoned. After a few weeks we had saved enough money to prepare for our next big passage — the brief offshore run to the Dry Tortugas.

Molly's sister, Lori, joined us during her spring break from Harvard Law School. Molly showed Lori around the boat, and after she stowed her gear we gathered in the cockpit. Lori was shocked at the things we didn't have aboard.

"You don't have a VHF radio, a life raft, or any medical supplies other than Band-Aids?" Lori asked, more than a bit surprised.

"No, I'm sorry, Lori," I confessed. "But don't worry, we do have *a* life jacket."

"You have *one* life jacket?" Lori couldn't tell if I was joking.

"Yes," I said. "I guess it will be quite a fight to see who grabs it first if we start to sink."

To her credit, Lori's resolve to sail was unshaken, and we set off on March 22, 1980. The Dry Tortugas consist of a few small islands 70 miles west of Key West. We had an exhilarating sail as a strong easterly wind whisked *Jeanne* along at hull speed. Our navigation proved accurate when Molly spotted land dead ahead, just below the setting sun.

We sailed up the twisting channel and smartly anchored off Garden Key. (When you anchor under sail, you have a fifty-fifty chance that things will go according to plan and you will impress everyone in the harbor. Unfortunately, the other half of the time you make a complete fool of yourself.)

Fort Jefferson, a national monument, occupies almost all of Garden Key. The massive fort was strategically erected as part of Lincoln's blockade of the South during the Civil War. The fort has an enviable record of never having had to fire a shot in confrontation with the enemy. In fact, the fort's only claim to fame is that Samuel Mudd was imprisoned there. Dr. Mudd was the rogue who followed his Hippocratic oath to the extreme when he set John Wilkes Booth's broken leg after Booth shot President Lincoln. Some forts are just destined for goodness; while imprisoned, Dr. Mudd distinguished himself during a yellow fever epidemic and was granted an early pardon.

We spent several days exploring the fort, swimming, snorkeling, and just plain relaxing. On April Fool's Day we set off for Key West. The wind was still blowing out of the east, and we were obliged to pound into it. *Jeanne,* God knows I loved her, unfortunately went to windward like a beached manatee, and we spent a long day and night tacking eastward.

In the morning I had to admit to my fearless crew that, although we were not lost, I wasn't quite sure where we were. I was paranoid about sailing onto the reefs of the Marquesas, just west of Key West, so I decided to heave-to while I determined our position.

While Molly had worked in Key West, I studied celestial navigation. I had most of the required equipment, including a sextant, an almanac, and the sight reduction tables. What I didn't have was an accurate timepiece. Precise time is fundamental to celestial navigation. Roughly speaking, a 4-second error in time causes a one-mile error in position.

The clock I used to time my sights was a windup alarm clock that not only wasn't accurate, but did not even have a second hand!

When the minute hand came up on the hour, I had Molly begin to count: one, one-thousand; two, one-thousand; etc. I took a round of sights and Lori recorded the time. I then solemnly retired below to unravel the black magic of celestial navigation.

An hour later I returned to the cockpit. "Well, where are we?" Molly asked.

"Well, baby, we're either in Tampa Bay or Puerto Rico — something must have gone wrong. But don't worry," I continued, trying to sound as though I knew what I was talking about. "At noon I'll take a meridian passage shot and find our latitude, and then . . ."

"Hey, there's a shrimp boat," Lori yelled. "Why don't we hail him and ask him where we are?"

I was disgusted with such a cowardly, unseamanlike, but very logical plan. Fortunately for my bruised ego, Lori and Molly were unable to raise the attention of the captain. An hour later, around noon, I was on the spot. I carefully measured the sun's maximum altitude over a period of about 20 minutes. Then I calculated our latitude and, wonder of wonders, it corresponded with my dead-reckoning position. I had a reasonable idea of where we were! We set the genoa and drove *Jeanne* hard to windward. We anchored in Key West an hour before Lori's flight back to Boston.

The post office was one of our daily destinations in Key West. We not only checked for mail, we usually had breakfast there as well. Cold, fresh water was a tough commodity for boats in the anchorage to come by, and we discovered that the post office had the best drinking fountain in town. Each morning before we rowed ashore, Molly loaded up her backpack with a box of Wheaties, a couple of bowls, and a supply of powdered milk. After checking for mail, we'd mix our cereal at the fountain, sit on the front steps, and discuss the day's activities.

Shortly after our return to Key West, we received a letter from my mom. I read it while eating my Wheaties, and I was surprised at the serious tone. Mom wrote that she was weary — weary of commuting to work 40 miles each way on the freeway; weary of long, dark northern winters; and most important, weary of business. For four years she'd skillfully managed the family business, and although the business was currently prospering, it hadn't always been that way. After assuming the reins when my father died, she was immediately confronted by a brutal recession that bankrupted many small businesses. She had remortgaged the house to meet payroll, and placated impatient bankers with her charm. Her ever-present smile was only a mask for fierce determination. She had been obsessed with succeeding and not blowing what my father had worked so hard to achieve. And she did succeed, but she was lonely and tired. She needed a change, and she had an interesting proposition for Molly and me.

She wanted us to sell *Jeanne,* and together the three of us would buy a larger boat and sail to distant shores. Initially, Molly and I were overwhelmed. "What a great idea," we thought. Infatuated with the thought of a larger boat and the proper gear, I called home and told Mom we would set sail for Miami within a week and put *Jeanne* on the market.

That evening we went into Key West to celebrate our good fortune. We had a few beers at The Bull, one of the raunchiest bars in town. Listening to a lousy country band, we discussed Mom's proposal in a different light — a mother, a son, and a girlfriend? What an odd trio, especially cooped up in the small confines of a yacht.

"It's going to require a lot of effort on everyone's part to make it work," I said to Molly.

"Oh, John, we'll make the effort. This is a great opportunity."

"You're right, Molly, but it's going to be especially tough for you, living with my mother."

"Don't worry, Johnny, I get along well with your mother. We'll work it out."

Before we left for Miami, we reserved a slip at the old Naval Dock along the waterfront. Molly and I had been living at anchor or at sea (except when we were aground) for the better part of five months. We relished the thought of hosing the boat down with fresh water and going into town without worrying about the anchor dragging.

Unfortunately, the morning after we sailed into our slip, President Carter decided to use the old Naval Dock as a modern-day Ellis Island. Thousands of Cubans fleeing Castro's tyranny arrived at the dock as the infamous "Mariel Boat Lift" began. Molly and I were afraid to leave the boat for even a second. Key West was chaotic as boats of every description poured into the harbor, loaded to the gunwales with freedom-seeking Cubans. Cuban-Americans also swarmed into town, hoping to find a long-sought relative somewhere among the throngs of refugees.

Molly and I were relieved to reach out into Hawk Channel and point *Jeanne*'s bow to the northeast. Sudden squalls plagued our passage to Long Key, but we proficiently shortened sail every time a towering cumulus reared its ugly thunderhead. We were both a bit melancholy — after all, this was our final passage aboard *Jeanne.* We anchored in Long Key Bight, halfway between Key West and Miami, on April 29, 1980.

The Bight is quite shallow, and, despite our 4-foot draft, we were forced to anchor more than a mile offshore. The previous night we had burned the last wick for the kerosene lamp, our only light source aboard. After several improvised wicks failed to hold a light, we decided to row ashore and buy a new one. The nearest marine store was on Lower Matecumbe Key, a 3-mile row from where *Jeanne* lay anchored.

Jeanne's faithful dinghy deserves mention. A dependable dinghy is as indispensable to the cruising sailor as a car is to the suburban family. Ours was an inexpensive, bright orange Sportyak. Although it was blunt bowed and just 6 feet long, it rowed well and supported a heavy load. The manufacturer claimed it was unsinkable, and we were about to see if he was right.

We paid out 70 feet of anchor rode for a very safe scope and then piled into the dinghy. It took almost an hour to reach the western tip of Matecumbe Key. Fortunately, the marine store had just the wick we needed. We stopped for a quick beer and hurried back to the dinghy because it had begun to rain. I rowed at a good clip, hoping to dodge the brewing thunderstorm.

We were about halfway between the shore and the boat when the rain stopped abruptly and the light breeze disappeared. An eerie calm enveloped the Bight — but it was only the calm before the storm. When the wind returned, it was warm and wet and had shifted 180 degrees to the northwest. The wind speed increased in frightening degrees; first to 15 knots, then to 30 knots, then to 50 knots, and then — we learned later — to 70 knots! The sky went from gray to black, as black as a moonless night, and a full-blown tornado raged out of the northwest directly for Long Key Bight. Molly and I were trapped in our 6-foot, plastic dinghy!

The powerful wind churned up almost instant 6- to 8-foot waves. We were driven seaward, toward Cuba. Violent gusts lifted the dinghy completely out of the water and hurled it through the air while I futilely swung the oars. Molly bailed frantically as one wave after another swamped the dinghy.

"We're gonna make it, Molly. Just keep bailing — it'll be OK. It's got to pass. I know it will. We just have to hold on and keep bailing."

"Johnny, damn it, we're swamped. I can't stay ahead of the water. Oh, God, I don't want to die."

The dinghy was no longer being thrown through the air; instead it was completely submerged and rode just below the surface of the water. For some reason it didn't sink, and somehow it remained upright. Molly clung tenaciously to the painter and I rowed wildly, but it was like rowing underwater; I could not stop us from being driven out to sea.

"Johnny," Molly cried. "Oh, baby, I'm glad we're together — I mean, if this is it, baby, at least we are together."

"Molly, I'll love you forever, but damn it, the ocean is not going to get us yet, not yet. Just hold on — whatever you do, don't let go of that line."

During a momentary lull I noticed the color of the water change from green to brown; miraculously we were passing over a sandbar! I lashed the painter around my waist, gave the end to Molly, and plunged into the water. It was our only chance. The water came up to my chest in the troughs of the waves, but even during the crests I was able to keep my feet firmly planted on the ground by ducking underwater. I was the Rock of Gibraltar — nothing was going to move me. Finally, the tornado passed over the Bight.

As fast as the storm emerged it disappeared, and a surreal peacefulness returned to the Bight. Slowly, I pulled the dinghy ashore. The oars were gone, victims of the storm. When visibility improved, we were incredibly relieved to see that *Jeanne* was still in the Bight. She hadn't been driven out to sea or piled up on the beach. She had dragged anchor about a half mile, but except for a tattered jib which we had left on deck, she looked OK.

During the ten minutes of terror, Molly and I both had seen our lives pass before us. We all react to a brush with death differently. Although we had been rattled to the core and thoroughly humbled, we held no malice toward the sea. If anything, the tornado only served to strengthen our resolve to continue with our plans to sail around the world. Maybe it was King Neptune's way of saying, "OK, you landlubbers, you're sincere in your quest and you've passed your first test."

2

A New Epoch

*W*HEN WE ARRIVED IN Miami, we immediately put *Jeanne* up for sale. She sparkled after we varnished the brightwork, waxed the hull, and thoroughly cleaned the interior. We even purchased a used British Seagull outboard engine. The Seagull was loud, burned oil, and coughed up more fumes than a chainsmoker. Still, it was a luxury to move *Jeanne* forward without raising a sail.

I was attempting to sell *Jeanne* myself and save the 10 percent brokerage commission, but I was too emotionally attached to the old girl. When interested buyers criticized her, their barbs stung me personally. Another, more pressing problem was that the Seagull did not have a reverse gear, and there was no way to stop the boat in a hurry. Returning to the dock after a test sail with a potential buyer was always a bit nerve-wracking.

If things went well, I casually lassoed a piling with the stern line as *Jeanne* eased into her slip. Then I quickly but calmly snubbed the line and brought the boat to a smooth stop — the picture of seamanship. If things didn't go well, and, for example, I missed the piling, the ensuing crash landing and desperate shouts of "Fend off, fend off!" rarely impressed the buyer. I finally listed *Jeanne* with a yacht broker.

Speaking of yacht brokers, few took Molly and me seriously as we began our search for what we nicknamed "the ultimate boat." Only one broker, Johnny Woods of Ft. Lauderdale, wasn't put off by my long, scraggly hair, Molly's sixteenish looks, and our bold talk about sailing around the world. Johnny was young and eager to sell boats, and he tirelessly escorted us around town, showing us one boat after another.

Our financing scheme seemed simple enough. When *Jeanne* sold, Molly and I would supply the down payment for the new boat and Mom would arrange financing. Mom was obliged to return to Detroit periodically to keep tabs on her business, and Molly and I figured we would work whenever we had a lengthy stay in port. Naively, we also thought we could help defray the cost of cruising by conducting occasional charters en route. However, we came to learn the two fundamental rules of cruising the hard way: first, it will cost far more than you ever imagined; and second, you can't let that stop you from going.

Our experiences aboard *Jeanne* helped shape our parameters for selecting a new boat. We definitely wanted a fiberglass hull for ease of maintenance, between 35 and 40 feet long. The boat also had to be sensibly designed and well constructed, but we were not limiting ourselves to traditional designs. In fact, the frustration of trying to con *Jeanne* to windward convinced us that a large fin keel and skeg-protected rudder just might be the best hull shape. We also needed private accommodations, either in the form of a center cockpit or an aft cockpit with an aft cabin off to one side. There was one final prerequisite, and, unfortunately, it spoiled a lot of our fun — the ultimate boat also had to be affordable. For that reason we concentrated our search on used boats.

We were intrigued by a bargain-priced ketch built in Taiwan. A closer inspection revealed why she was such a bargain; she was a rotting mess. We looked at a Canadian-built Whitby 42, but it seemed a bit stodgy and was priced out of our league. We went so far as to test sail an Allied Mistress. The 39-foot Allied was a well-constructed center-cockpit ketch, both affordable and practical. But it just wasn't right. A sailboat is like a lover — there has to be that initial spark of romance. You know you've found the right boat when you look at her lines and feel your heart rate quicken. It's absurd, but true.

Molly and I were frustrated, and we discussed our alternatives endlessly. Sitting in *Jeanne*'s cockpit, I said, "The Allied is really practical, Molly," but she just sneered. I didn't have a chance to pursue the point because Johnny Woods pulled up. He stepped out of his car and said, "You guys, I have a 'must see' boat for you."

The boat was in Ft. Lauderdale, moored well up the New River.

"She's called *L'Ouranos*," Johnny explained, trying to emulate a sophisticated French accent. "She was built in France and she's fresh from a transatlantic passage. I don't know," he continued, "there is something about her — she's kind of sexy." I groaned and wondered what Johnny's idea of a sexy boat would look like.

Sometimes there is more than just a spark — *L'Ouranos* cast a spell that seduced Molly and me like an overpowering aphrodisiac. She was hidden behind a residence as we drove up, but, even from the street, it was easy to spot her towering spar above the trees. We hopped out of the car and dashed behind the house to the canal. "Wow!" I said to Molly. She just smiled. *L'Ouranos* was sleek, she was unmistakably European, and she was not at all like most of the clumsy cruising boats we'd been looking at. With her near-flush deck and low profile, I thought to myself, "I'll be damned — Johnny's right. She is sexy."

Technically speaking, *L'Ouranos* was built by Jeanneau of France and saddled with the silly trade name of 'Gin Fizz Sloop. Her dimensions were: 37 feet 6 inches LOA; 12 feet 2 inches beam; 6 feet 2 inches draft; 6,000 pounds ballast; and 15,400 pounds displacement with her fin keel and flat bottom. She was shaped like an around-the-buoys racing boat. She looked fast just tied to the dock.

Modern design or not, *L'Ouranos* was definitely constructed for bluewater sailing. Her hull was heavily laid up — a 1-inch hull plug attested to that. Her standing rigging was oversized, and most of her equipment first-rate. Also, her interior arrangement was perfect for the three of us, because she had an oversized lazarette (the French call it an aft cabin) with a double berth for Molly and me. Yet, in the end, it was her irresistible French charm that convinced us we'd finally found the ultimate boat.

Buying *L'Ouranos* proved almost as challenging as finding her. We had to wait until *Jeanne* finally sold before we could make an offer. Once the French-Canadian owners accepted our bid, Johnny Woods had to convince them to pay U.S. duty before we could legally transfer ownership. Also, financing a used boat during the recession of 1980 was quite difficult, and we were forced to accept high interest rates and steep monthly payments. We finally moved aboard in early July.

Many sailors subscribe to the superstition that the name of a boat should never be changed, but I'm not one of them. *L'Ouranos,* the French version of the god of the sky, was a lovely name, but it wasn't our name, and besides, none of us could pronounce it with much flair. Throwing caution to the wind, Molly ruthlessly scrubbed off the ornate lettering and boldly splashed our new name across the transom, *Epoch*. Indeed, we were truly launching a new "Epoch."

Changing the name was easy; refitting the boat to sail around the world wasn't. *Epoch* was well equipped, but a lot of her gear was worn out. I was still a bungling non-handyman, and despite the very best of intentions, I made many alterations I came to regret.

For starters, I replaced a supposedly lethal (but wonderfully convenient) butane stove with a smelly, cranky, and inefficient kerosene model. Next, I traded a six-man Zodiac inflatable dinghy and outboard for a fiberglass tender that was nearly impossible to stow. But my worst mistake was to convert the electrical system from a perfectly adequate European 6-volt system to an American 12-volt system. Through 10,000 miles of cruising we were never sure what light corresponded to what switch, and we set a record by wrecking seven batteries in less than a year!

Fortunately, *Epoch* was a forgiving boat, and, to our credit, we did make some worthwhile improvements. We installed an Aries self-steering wind vane, rigged a more efficient slab-reefing system, and installed new seacocks on all through-hull fittings. By the end of July we were ready to commence our journey, and what a journey we planned. We chose an indirect route to the Caribbean, which we saw as the first stage of our eventual circumnavigation. We planned to first sail north along the East Coast of the U.S. to North Carolina, then offshore to Bermuda, and finally south to the Caribbean. This wayward route had three objectives. First, it would give us time to master our new boat while we were still within hollering distance of the U.S. coast. Second, it was an interesting and relatively safe way to pass the summer hurricane season. Finally, by sailing offshore to Bermuda in the fall, we would test our mettle and see if we were capable of carrying out our ambitious dreams.

The three of us were giddy when we powered out of Miami's Government Cut, bound north. Shortly after we cleared the inlet, a sudden summer squall forced us to reef the mainsail, but *Epoch* held her course. The squall passed quickly, and the stars that replaced the thunderheads gave me indication that maybe, just maybe, we could sail clear around the world. In the morning I was ready to impress the crew with my revamped celestial navigation skills.

I carefully took a round of sun sights and went below to plot the results. When I plotted the line of position, it coincided with my dead-reckoning position. "I'll just snatch the noon sight in a couple of hours, which will give us latitude, advance this morning's LOP, and presto, we'll have our position," I explained to Mom. Mastering celestial navigation was vital to our plans, and I was determined to become a good navigator. Just before noon the sun reached its zenith in the sky, and I recorded the altitude with my plastic sextant. I worked and reworked the figures; something had to be wrong. In just over 24 hours of sailing my dead reckoning was 75 miles off!

"Well, where are we?" came the impatient shouts from the cockpit.

"Well, just hold on a minute," I grumbled.

"How is the Gulf Stream affecting us?" Molly asked.

"Oh, ya," I thought to myself. "You jerk." I had completely forgotten about the swift, north-setting Gulf Stream current. Three knots multiplied by 24 hours equals 72 miles, almost exactly the margin of my dead-reckoning error!

News of a tropical storm in the Caribbean persuaded us to call at historic, tourist-infested St. Augustine on the north Florida coast. The storm rapidly developed into a full-blown hurricane named Allen and caused extensive damage in the West Indies and along the Texas coast. We were prepared to take the *Epoch* as far inland as possible, but the hurricane didn't come our way.

While we were temporarily harbor-bound, we decided to haul the boat and paint the bottom. We hauled on August 9, and even though it was her 20th birthday, Molly worked diligently all day. When the sun finally set, she looked very disappointed — she'd thought that I'd forgotten her birthday. But I hadn't, and after dinner, when we climbed back aboard, she met her present: a tiny, four-week-old kitten.

Molly was thrilled, and we all thought the idea of a ship's kitty was a good idea. That is, everyone but Kayla, as the kitty came to be called. He just didn't like the fact that he'd been shanghaied, and he sought vengeance whenever he could. Molly's hands were soon scarred from bites and scratches. Mom kept her distance after he delivered a dead mouse to her berth in the middle of the night. Strangely, Kayla tolerated me; maybe he thought we men had to stick together. Happy or not, Kayla became an official member of the crew as *Epoch* cleared St. Augustine and continued north.

We sailed in short, offshore hops to Savannah, Georgia; Charleston, South Carolina; and finally Wrightsville Beach, North Carolina. The *Epoch* was swift and seaworthy despite her mechanical flaws. We were enamored with her. It's amazing how quickly your status can change. Because we eschewed the monotony of the Intracoastal Waterway, every time we arrived in port most of the other yachtsmen were surprised to learn that we preferred to sail on the "outside." Just as we were beginning to feel smug about our seamanship, I blew our cover when we arrived in Wrightsville Beach.

A swift tidal current sets through the waterway, and I made a fool of myself trying to back the boat into a slip at a local marina. We careened

Jeanne L. Kretschmer at the helm.

from piling to piling, and I alternately screamed at Molly and Mom. Finally the marina manager, a white-haired curmudgeon, helped corral us in the middle of the slip.

"Maybe you should just go back where you came from, young man," he told me insultingly. "You'll never make it down the waterway to Florida."

"For your information, mister," Mom retorted, "we're going to Bermuda, and then around the world!"

"You gotta be kidding, lady — I mean, oh, Jesus . . . ." He wiped his brow, threw his hands up in the air, and stomped away.

The long-term weather forecast called for high pressure and west, northwest winds. We received an "all clear" from the National Hurricane Center on October 11, 1980, and later that morning the intrepid crew of the *Epoch* departed for Bermuda. We had stuffed six months' worth of provisions aboard, and we felt we were prepared for whatever the Atlantic Ocean had in store for us.

Bermuda, a tiny island archipelago of 20 square miles, stands alone,

660 miles east of Cape Hatteras, North Carolina. A brisk westerly sent *Epoch* surging along, and the low, sandy coastline quickly faded from view. I was a nervous wreck. I couldn't help but remember our misadventures in the Keys just months earlier: Were we truly ready for the North Atlantic? My stomach gave me the answer — *No*! I was miserably seasick for the first time in my life. Molly was also feeling a bit green, and we took turns at the stern rail. Fortunately, Mom was undaunted. Her stomach is cast in stainless steel, and as she says, "I don't buy that equilibrium nonsense. After seven childbirths, I'm certainly not going to get seasick." *Epoch* steered herself during the night, and in the morning Molly and I both found our sea legs.

The wind piped up to 30 knots and shifted astern. I dropped the mainsail, lowered and lashed the boom, and exchanged the genoa for the working jib. We reeled off three consecutive 150 mile, 24-hour runs. The sailing was exhilarating, and we settled into an effective routine. We kept an informal watch during the day and stood three-hour watches at night. I was the captain and navigator, Molly was our tireless helmsman, and Mom was an indomitable cook.

The strong westerly winds heaped up wild, rolling combers, and *Epoch* was akin to a downhill skier as she schussed down the waves. The weather began to change on October 14, as towering cumulus clouds gave way to spreading layers of gray overcast. The barometer accelerated what had been a steady decline, and the pressure plunged to 990 millibars. During the ugly morning of October 15, the wind backed abruptly to the east and piped up to gale force. Luckily, I obtained one last sextant sight before the sky completely clouded over. We were just 42 miles west of Bermuda.

I was confident that we could beat to windward through the night and make port in the morning. We all knew it would be a miserable slug, but the thought of a hot shower and a cold beer just a day away put new vigor in the crew. All through the night we relentlessly pounded into the rising wind and waves. First light, October 16, revealed a frightening storm-tossed ocean. We were startled to spot a rusty containership nearby. I hailed the ship on the VHF radio. Captain Rodriguez was most informative and quite concerned. When we compared positions, we discovered that we had actually lost ground during the night and were still 50 miles from Bermuda. When I told him that my crew consisted of my mother and my girlfriend, he was astounded and offered to lower his longboat and send me over some extra rum! His advice was: "Never take a woman to sea!"

He told us that the gale was forecast to persist all day. *Epoch,* our beloved but flat-bottomed, fin-keeled race boat, had made appalling leeway during the night. I decided it was crazy to continue to pound into the seas, so we hove-to instead. We tied in the third reef on the mainsail and hoisted the storm jib. With her sails backwinded, *Epoch* was like a caged bird, but she rode the seas with surprising buoyancy. She didn't head into the seas as well as *Jeanne* had, and the motion was quite uncomfortable, but I felt secure in the Force 8 conditions.

Another day slipped by, and Molly summed up our feelings with her log entry: "The day was gray and the night just a darker shade." While Molly and I battled the storm, Mom battled our cantankerous kerosene stove. Despite the violent motion below, she kept the crew well fed throughout the tempest. On October 17 the storm reached its apex, and I estimated the winds at 50 knots and the seas at 25 feet. I worried about the strain on the rig and the battering the hull was taking, and decided we had to change tactics. It was time to give up any hopes of making Bermuda and run from the storm.

Running downwind required constant vigilance at the helm to keep *Epoch* from rounding up and broaching. The Aries wind vane wasn't up to the task; instead, we stood exhausting two-hour tricks at the helm. Thirty-six hours later, the gale overran us and left *Epoch* and her exhausted crew becalmed, about 200 miles southwest of Bermuda.

The 200-mile figure was purely hypothetical, because I hadn't taken a sight in days. But when a light westerly emerged, we decided to give Bermuda one more try, and pointed the bow to the east. Two days later, as *Epoch* rode on the crest of a swell, Molly spotted the faint outline of Bermuda on the horizon. We arrived on October 21. We had been at sea for 11 days.

Bermuda seemed like a fairyland, especially after the trials of our turbulent passage. We tarried for a couple of weeks. We wandered through the pastel-shaded cottages of quaint St. George, zipped into busy Hamilton on mopeds, and even ran a few day charters on the sly. Ronald Reagan was swept into office on a landslide, but American politics, just 700 miles away, seemed strangely remote. Winter in the North Atlantic was fast approaching, and on November 7 we cleared customs and departed for St. Thomas in the tropical U.S. Virgin Islands.

The 800-mile passage due south was the antithesis of the boisterous Bermuda run. Light, fluky winds slowed our progress, and celestial navigation was next to impossible in the constant overcast conditions. The sun made a few cameo appearances, quickly darting from one cloud to the next. Luckily, I was ready with my sextant several times and made the most out of a handful of sights. At dawn on November 15, Molly spotted St. Thomas dead ahead. It's amazing how much easier a passage is the second time around.

The Virgin Islands were thrust up from the floor of the ocean with the charter-boat industry in mind. The hundred or so islands in the 40-mile-long chain are a magical place to sail. The countless anchorages are almost all deep and well protected and fringed by sandy beaches.

The islands are cooled by the steady northeast tradewinds, and if there is one problem with the Virgins, it is that too many people have found paradise. During the winter season, the islands are almost overrun with charter boats, and *Epoch* had a few close encounters with neophyte sailors on holiday.

One evening, after exploring the rock formations called The Baths, we anchored off aptly named Colison Point on the northwestern shore of Virgin Gorda. It was a cool, rainy night, and we were below reading. Molly happened to glance up through the companionway and noticed a large sailboat very close to our stern. She dashed into the cockpit just in time to fend off a 50-foot charter boat and prevent it from crushing our steering vane. The boat had dragged anchor and was marauding through the crowded anchorage.

Another night we dropped the hook in Caneel Bay, off the Rockefeller Resort in St. John. It's one of the loveliest but most congested anchorages in the Virgins. Prudence dictates a short scope on your anchor rode, but one boat, obviously a bareboat charterer, inconsiderately paid out an excessive amount of scope. In the middle of the night, when the tide changed and the wind came up, boats began to swing around. The charter boat was like a battering ram on the end of a pendulum. As it careened from one anchored boat to another all night long, we were awakened by vicious shouts, until finally the *Epoch* was its next victim. I yelled and hollered at the chubby captain, imploring him to shorten his scope, but he refused, claiming that he had anchored first. I was furious and threatened to break his neck before Mom and Molly insisted we move to the outer anchorage.

We returned to St. Thomas, and Molly and Mom abandoned ship for the Christmas holidays. Mom returned to Detroit and Molly attended a family gathering in southern Illinois. Kayla and I were responsible for the *Epoch*. Challenged by the thought of singlehanded sailing and eager to leave the crowds of St. Thomas, I set sail for St. John.

It was only a 15-mile sail back to Caneel Bay, a couple of hours at most, and I didn't bother to engage the steering vane before I left. I skirted Long Point and set a course for Current Cut. Current Cut is a narrow, reef-fringed passage between southeastern St. Thomas and

Great St. James Island and a popular shortcut to Pillsbury Sound and the Sir Francis Drake Channel. Two approaching sailboats were holding to the starboard side of the cut, and it was obvious we would pass port to port close aboard. Suddenly the morning's Cheerios triggered my bowels and I had an unbearable urge to relieve myself. "The urge will surely pass," I thought, but then came the cramps. We were nearly abreast of the boats — I had two alternatives: to leave the wheel and dash below, which was unthinkable in the narrow cut; or to go in my shorts. Then I spotted Kayla's litterbox in the corner of the cockpit. I quickly grabbed it, and, to the utter horror of the sunbathers on the nearby boats, I found relief. From that moment on Kayla worshipped me.

Mom and Molly returned after New Year's, and the restless crew of the *Epoch* sailed across the notorious Anegada Passage to St. Martin in the Leeward Islands. We spent weeks winding our way south through the Leewards. First to French and Dutch St. Martin, then on to St. Barts, St. Kitts, Montserrat, and Guadeloupe. The Leeward Islands are an ideal cruising ground. Each island is only a day's sail away from the next, but each has a history, culture, and character all its own.

However, trouble was brewing aboard the *Epoch,* even in paradise. Although we feasted on fresh baguette in the morning, soaked up tropical sunshine during the day, and drank good, cheap French wines at night, we could not ease the growing friction among the crew. Bridging the generation gap between a mother, son, and girlfriend was a full-time job. In port I felt guilty leaving Mom behind whenever Molly and I went off alone. Molly, on the other hand, seemed a bit resentful that our time together was metered, especially after the intimacy of the Keys. Both Mom and Molly were patient with me and each other. We were really trying to make the cruising life work; maybe we were trying too hard.

As a sailing team we had few troubles and learned to handle *Epoch* confidently. Any differences we had in port seemed to evaporate out at sea. That is why we often put to sea after only a couple of days in a new port. "We're spending two years in the islands — you're missing so much," was the theme often echoed to us by other cruisers. Maybe we were, but once at sea we were content. From Guadeloupe we charted a return course to St. Thomas to make a few repairs to the boat. With the *Epoch* shipshape, on February 1, 1981, we set off across the Caribbean, bound for Panama and the Pacific Ocean.

According to the pilot chart, a small-scale wind and weather guide, we expected a downwind sleigh ride for most of the 1,100-mile passage. The tradewinds didn't let us down, but once again my mechanical skills did. The second day out of St. Thomas, the fuel lines on the kerosene stove clogged up. Employing my usual delicate touch, I snapped both copper lines trying to clean them. This infuriated Mom. "Damn, Johnny, why do we always have to do things the hard way?" We were forced to cook in a charcoal pot in the cockpit, and, needless to say, we ate a lot of cold tuna and crackers for the next seven days.

The northeast tradewinds reached gale force on February 4. Steering a steady course before the wind was exhausting. Even with just the storm jib set, *Epoch* routinely pegged the knotmeter at 10 knots. I feared that she might round up after surfing down a wave and broach or possibly capsize. I decided to lower the storm jib and run under bare poles, but that proved to be a mistake.

Although our speed slowed dramatically, steering was even more demanding because the helm became dangerously unresponsive. One nasty wave emphasized my tactical error by crashing over the stern. Water poured into *Epoch*'s large cockpit and filled it above the seats. The aft cabin was flooded. One marauding wave had turned our orderly world into chaos. But we didn't panic. Instead, we sprang into action. I gave Molly the helm and she steered a course to take the seas on the quarter. Mom immediately started to pump the bilge, and I rushed forward to reset the storm jib. Once the water was out of the boat, we were out of danger. We steered conscientiously throughout the night, and, luckily, the gale blew itself out after 24 hours.

Tired, hungry and ready for port, we spotted the breakwater off Colon, the Caribbean terminus of the Panama Canal, on February 8, 1981. Even without hot food and after weathering a full gale, we had still managed a smart passage by averaging 138 miles per day.

Although Colon is a dangerous, decaying city, Panama still seemed most exotic. After filling out pages of customs forms, we tied up at a yacht club within the U.S. military compound. Just 9 degrees above the equator, the tropical air hung heavy as we sipped beer at the club bar. The shifty characters eavesdropping on our sea stories and eyeing Mom and Molly looked as though they had just stepped out of a Gabriel Garcia Marquez novel.

After we made arrangements to transit the Canal, we took a taxi into town to purchase fresh food at the "mercado." Gangs of young boys loitered on every street corner, and the driver explained Panama's staggering unemployment problem. Stopped at a traffic light, the driver suddenly poked my shoulder and pointed to the car in front of us. A young boy was reaching into the car and grabbing for a lady's necklace. The driver ordered Molly and Mom to duck down in the back seat and then squealed around the car, running the red light. "It's just no good," the driver said, exasperated. "You Americans should take the Canal back."

That sentiment was repeated by many Panamanians we spoke with. The treaty, which had just gone into effect, granted sovereignty of the Canal to Panama. According to terms of the treaty, employees of the Canal suddenly found themselves working for Panamanian wages and benefits instead of American. The result to the economy was staggering and immediate. The Panamanian people needed a villain and Jimmy Carter fit the bill. Stuffed Jimmy Carter dolls hung in effigy from high-rise buildings. Poor President Carter was a villain all right, the villain of an old cliche: "The road to hell is paved with good intentions."

In spite of Panama's depressing economic condition, transiting the Canal was still a thrill. With a couple of extra hands along to meet the crew requirements, we negotiated six locks and traversed Gatun Lake, for a total distance of 45 miles across the Isthmus. We reached the Pacific terminus late in the evening. Vasco de Balboa could not have been more excited than I was to see the vast reaches of the Pacific, illuminated by a brilliant full moon.

We took a mooring at the Balboa Yacht Club and attended to several serious problems on the boat. First, we had to buy a new stove, which was quite challenging in Panama. We searched all over Panama City before we finally purchased two ancient-looking kerosene-wick burners made in Red China circa 1920. I wired the Chinese burners into the old stove frame and honestly expected them to last about a week. Our homemade electrical system was also acting up. We were frequently without lights, which is not only inconvenient, but also dangerous, especially in the shipping lanes around Panama.

I hired a Panamanian electrician, and he was a complete hack as he shorted out the few remaining circuits that still worked. However, not all short circuits were electrical; more and more often I was losing my patience and temper. After one outburst, when I hollered at Molly and nearly threw Diego, the electrician, overboard, Mom decided we needed a crew meeting. We checked into the Panama Hilton.

Over an expensive but dreadful meal, we discussed our future plans.

"Johnny," Mom asked me, "do you think *Epoch* is up to the 4,000-mile passage to the Marquesas Islands?"

"I don't know, Mom. But one thing is for sure; once we start, if we decide to turn back, it will be dead to windward."

Mom and I were skirting the issue. The real issue was not the boat but the crew, and Mom and I knew it.

"Look, kids, let's be honest with each other — the *Epoch*'s not the problem, we are. We are just not making it as a threesome. It's a long way around the world, and I think we could all use a change."

Molly and I began to protest, but Mom waved her hand and we shut up. "Hey, kids, don't be blue. You have both been so very patient with an old gal like me. You've shown me a wonderful time, and, besides, more adventures lie ahead. We sure are not going to leave the *Epoch* here in Panama. What do you say we head up the coast to California? We'll reevaluate our plans then."

Once we had a set destination, shipboard morale improved. We were all both relieved and a little disappointed; we'd already sailed 5,000 miles, but we'd altered plans at a crucial crossroads. We finally put the electrical system in order and set sail. Our first destination on the Pacific coast was Costa Rica.

We beat through choppy seas off the appropriately named Punta Mala (Bad Point), on Panama's Peninsula de Azuero. Once we cleared the point, we tacked northwest for Costa Rica. A couple days of hard sailing later, we dropped the hook in the Gulf of Dulce, in front of the jungle-surrounded village of Golfito. Golfito must be one of the hottest places on the planet, but Captain Tom always kept a stock of Imperial (a local beer) on ice.

Captain Tom, who according to his own legend, piled up on the beach 20 years ago, owns a bar on the north shore of the bay. Tom is a peg-legged, aging hippie, who enthusiastically welcomes all visiting yachts. He serves his awful charcoaled monkey burgers and lots of Imperial to wash them down.

Mom had to return to Detroit, and, although she said it was for a board meeting, I think it was to avoid an expatriated American who had taken a fancy to her. Her friend lived next to the remains of Captain Tom's rotting, World War II subchaser in a shack on the beach. He claimed that he lived like a king on his monthly pension of $200. He also swore he was related to Captain Joshua Slocum. I have to admit, with his bald head and angular face, he did resemble the good captain.

Molly and I flew with Mom into San Jose, the capital, where she caught a connecting flight to the U.S. It was an unforgettable plane ride. The old prop plane rumbled down the runway and shook violently as it lifted into flight. The flight over the mountains was a rough one, and each time we encountered turbulence the locals would close their eyes, mumble prayers, and cross themselves. One crafty Indian had smuggled a few fighting cocks aboard, but he came to regret it. The cocks not only squawked every time the plane lurched, they also became miserably airsick. The puking chickens triggered mass sickness aboard the plane. It was surely the longest two-hour flight of our lives.

We spent a few days exploring hectic San Jose before returning to Golfito. Then we loaded up with fuel and water, jug by jug, and bid farewell to Captain Tom. Molly and I made sail for Puntarenas, Costa Rica's principal Pacific port, 300 miles to the north. Mom planned to rejoin us there. We anchored next to several American yachts in the shallow estuary behind the city.

Costa Rica is a haven of stability and democracy in strife-torn Central America. Imagine a country that boasts about having more schoolteachers than policemen! The country is prosperous and the people are friendly. Molly became a hero of sorts in Puntarenas when she participated in an otherwise all-male 10-mile road race. Although she tied for last place, she was awarded a special trophy and had her picture in the newspaper.

Costa Rica is also blessed with a diverse and beautiful geography. The government has preserved large tracts of land through an extensive and well-maintained national park system. We rented a beat-up pickup truck and traveled widely, camping most nights. We could have remained in Costa Rica a long time, but when Mom returned in early April she had bad news.

Her personal tax bill turned out to be much higher than she had anticipated, and, as a result, our cruising budget was suddenly, severely crimped. Although I had earned a little pocket money by teaching celestial navigation (which, ironically, I was finally pretty good at) my meager earnings could not replenish our empty cruising coffers. We decided to return to the U.S. as directly as possible, and although we were on the Pacific coast, Miami was still the nearest American port. Once back in the States, Molly and I would go to work and assume the boat payments. Once again, the almighty dollar was taking the wind out of our sails.

We launched our preparations in earnest for the return trip, but before we left, a friend, an expatriated American in the electrical business, asked me to do a personal favor for him. Let's call him Joe. Joe had sold $15,000 worth of U.S.-manufactured equipment to a wealthy Costa Rican yachtsman. Costa Rica charges a 100 percent duty on any imported equipment. There is a loophole around the law, however. If the equipment is destined for a foreign yacht in transit, and that yacht leaves the country within a week, there is no duty at all.

Joe asked me if I would sign for the Satnav receiver, radar unit, and water desalinator to save his client $15,000. As we sipped a couple of Imperials, he assured me in his casual, soft-spoken way that this type of thing went on all the time in Central America. "There's nothing to worry about," he said. "Everything will be taken care of. And there will be a little something for you." Being young, innocent, and stupid I naively strolled down to the customs office and signed the import papers. That night, two bottles of expensive Scotch were anonymously delivered to the boat. As I poured a round of drinks, I felt like a character in a Jimmy Buffett song: just a little bit proud to be involved in a Banana Republic conspiracy.

The following day was departure day, and I rowed ashore to clear customs and obtain our "Zarpe" or exit papers. The young customs inspector was a fusspot, and he suspected that something was wrong with our papers. "Oh shit," I thought to myself, "this is it for sure." The clerk informed me that the Port Captain wanted to come aboard to inspect the new equipment. "Senor," he said smiling, "there is no problem. If you have the equipment on your boat you are free to leave, but if you do not, you owe us 300,000 Colons ($15,000)."

Although the clerk spoke excellent English, I mumbled, "No comprendo, no comprendo. Un momento, Senor," and I dashed out of the building. Sweat was running down my face. I ran across the street into a bar and demanded use of the telephone. I hastily dialed Joe's number and his wife answered the phone.

"Where the hell is Joe?" I screamed. She recognized my voice.

"He's not here. He's out of town today."

"The hell he is. You better find him because I'll be at your house in five minutes and if he's not there I'll burn it down!" I was furious.

I left the bar in a full sprint, and I didn't slow down for 2 miles as I ran across town to Joe's house. Joe's wife looked through the peephole. "He's not here," she whined. "I swear it."

"I'll break this door down," I screamed. The look on my face terrified her, and I heard her bolt the door. Then I started to climb vertically up the side of the house just like Spiderman. I knew Joe's office was on the second floor. When I was halfway up, he poked his head out of the window.

"I'll meet you at customs in 20 minutes," he said, sounding frightened.

Barely clinging to the windowsill, I yelled, "If you're not there, I'll kill you!" I dropped off the side of the house, nearly breaking my ankle, and stomped back to the customs office.

Joe was there, and, fortunately for him, so were Mom and Molly. He had obviously anticipated that we might run into problems, because he had saved the shipping boxes from the original equipment. The Port Captain was angry and impatient and so was I, but for different reasons. Joe's voice was shaking as he asked me to load the boxes into the dinghy.

He and the hefty Port Captain clambered in as well, and we rode very low in the water as I rowed out to the boat against the tidal current. Alongside, I pitched the heavy boxes aboard, and my two guests tumbled on deck as well.

Joe had stuffed the water desalinator box with an outdated air conditioner and another box with an old radio that looked like the model my grandparents had owned to listen to FDR delivering his fireside chats. Then he rattled off numerous statistics in Spanish and emphatically pointed to several graphs in the owner's manual. Amazingly, he convinced the Port Captain that this junk was the new, $15,000 equipment!

I rowed back to the fuel dock, and the Port Captain issued us a Zarpe and a warning: "Don't hurry back to Costa Rica, senor."

Joe tried to apologize. I grabbed him by his shirt collar and told him that, if I ever saw him again, I'd kill him. "You're overreacting," he told me, and he slipped two crisp $100 bills into my pocket. I released him and he hurried off toward the bar — he needed a drink.

3

Stormy Christening

MOLLY, WITH KEEN EYES, spotted Fowey Rocks Light Tower off the port bow. Soon Miami's skyline would decorate the horizon. The ocean's magic carpet, the Gulf Stream, was whisking us toward the final destination of our voyage aboard *Epoch*. I turned the wheel over to Molly and went below to write the final entry in the log. Propped in my familiar perch at the chart table, I studied the small-scale chart sprawled before me. I avoided fretting about the impending responsibility of land life looming just ahead. Instead, I followed the thin graphite line on the chart and savored the memories of our final passage.

In just five days, we had sailed from Puntarenas back to the Panama Canal Zone. Like old hands, we transited the Canal a second time, this time going west to east. In Colon, Mom left the boat once again and returned to Detroit. She arranged for her nephew to take her place on the passage to Miami. My young cousin, Johnny, was just out of high school and a real landlubber from the deserts of Nevada. Yet Johnny's father had been a Navy man in World War II, and like his father, Johnny took to the sea naturally.

While at the yacht club, we befriended a couple of aging hippies aboard a bright orange, high-sided sloop called *Tangerine*. John and Dennis had just returned from the San Blas Islands, and they insisted that we call there before rushing back to Miami. It turned out to be a superb suggestion.

The San Blas Islands, just 75 miles east of the Canal Zone, are Panama's link with a bygone age. The atoll-like islands are inhabited by the Cuna Indians. The Cunas are a short, feisty people who have valiantly resisted most temptations to conform to twentieth-century standards. Women dominate the tribal society and support their families by sewing and selling "molas." Molas are brightly colored layers of cloth intricately cut and sewn into outrageous designs. The handsome molas can be purchased for about a dollar in the islands, yet back in the U.S. or in Europe they fetch up to $100 apiece.

Visiting yachts are prime targets for the tenacious lady hucksters, who have most assuredly learned a few twentieth-century selling techniques. Before our anchor even touched the bottom, we were besieged by "pongas," dugout canoes, and before we knew it, we were the proud owners of at least 10 molas. If I hadn't finally put my foot down, Molly and Johnny might have decided to make a spinnaker out of molas. After two delightful weeks in the islands, we set sail for Cozumel, off Mexico's Yucatan peninsula.

The 1,000-mile run from San Blas to Cozumel is tricky because the western Caribbean is sprinkled with several small islands and many offshore banks and reefs. Precise navigation is paramount, but we had plenty of time to avoid the hazards; our progress was painstakingly slow. The wind was annoyingly light, and, although our fuel tanks were filled, we were unable to motor because our usually reliable Perkins diesel had joined the list of mechanical casualties.

The calm weather had an eerie feel. It was unusually muggy and humid, and the sea had a pronounced swell. Today I would immediately recognize the preliminary signs of a hurricane, but as *Epoch* slowly drifted north, the captain and crew blithesomely pressed on, ignorant of the tempest brewing.

On May 7, 1981, we were about 200 miles south of Grand Cayman Island and still several days from Cozumel. The weather deteriorated rapidly, and by dinner time we knew we were in for more than just another gale. Later we learned that we were skirted by the first hurricane of the year, *Arlene*.

Arlene was a minor hurricane with sustained winds of 70 knots at her center. But minor or not, it was a very frightening experience. Fortunately, the storm formed quickly, and, therefore, the accompanying seas were not of hurricane proportion. *Arlene* moved rapidly to the west from below Jamaica, and we were unmercifully pelted by driving rains and vicious, gusting winds for more than 36 hours. Unprotected at the helm, we stood one-hour watches. At times the rain felt as though it would puncture our foul-weather gear, and it was impossible to face the wind. Luckily, the storm veered off to the north before the eye came our way. Driven westward under bare poles, we covered almost 300 miles in a day and a half. However, by May 9, *Arlene* had overrun us, and *Epoch* was left becalmed and bobbing on miserable swells.

The calm after the storm was maddening. Unable to motor, we were in sight of Cozumel's tantalizing coastline, thirsting for a cold beer, for 20 hours before we finally reached the anchorage off San Miguel. Cozumel had been severely battered by *Arlene,* and many local yachts had been destroyed. We were lucky to have ridden out the storm with plenty of sea room.

The Port Captain was a crook, and he thought he had a sucker in a twenty-two-year-old captain. He insisted that we had illegally entered the country by not having a pilot to guide us in, and, therefore, we owed him the $50 pilot's fee. I refused to pay what was an obvious bribe, and we never did officially clear customs. In fact, we stayed just long enough to reprovision and catch Montezuma's (or Port Captain's) revenge. When Cozumel dipped below the horizon astern, we were only 500 miles from Miami.

Molly cried out that she had spotted the markers leading into Biscayne Bay. She knew her way through the narrow channel, or at least I thought she did. "Thump, thump, thump." The chart was jarred off the desk. I dashed up into the cockpit as *Epoch* listed to starboard. Molly, at the helm, had a silly expression on her face. "Well, captain, it looks like we're hard aground. I guess that means we must be back in Miami."

On the passage up from Panama, Molly and I had decided to use the *Epoch* as the base for a sailing/navigation school. Our 7,500-mile cruise had taught us many lessons, lessons invariably learned the hard way. There had to be a better way. The school we envisioned would teach potential bluewater sailors the practical aspects of cruising — celestial navigation, diesel maintenance, etc., etc. In other words, all the eventual problems that stalled our voyage. Of course, it was a bit ironic that the dropout kid himself would want to start a school, of all things, but I launched the enterprise with spirit.

Mom helped us arrange a bank loan for a little seed capital, and Molly and I were in business. We hired a diesel mechanic and a former

RAF pilot to write course manuals and teach on a part-time basis. I also convinced my brother, Tom, to move to Florida and become my partner. We decided to locate the school in Ft. Lauderdale, the yachting mecca of the South. We rented and renovated a storefront on 17th Street Causeway, and on September 15, 1981, The Navigation School opened for business.

We anticipated making money in two ways. First, we offered week-long seminars in celestial, coastal, and electronic navigation, and we also conducted weekly, big-boat sailing lessons aboard *Epoch*. Second, we planned to produce income by marketing our courses as home-study manuals. We placed ads in major sailing publications and attended many boat shows promoting the school. The seminars caught on quickly in South Florida, but the home-study concept was a disaster. We originally projected modest sales of 20 courses a month; a steady home-study income was the potential profit margin for the school. The sorry truth was that the home-study market did not exist, and in the two years we operated the school we sold a paltry total of 17 courses!

Even though we ran a tight ship and worked long hours, we were barely keeping our heads above water. The seminars covered our expenses, and we branched out and conducted classes in New York, Houston, and Miami. We also tried other things to bring money in, and The Navigation School became a clearinghouse for yacht deliveries and navigational charters. Local sailors loved to stop in and chat; the school was the Turkish Smoke House of sailing. We made many friends, but precious little money.

I became increasingly disenchanted with business; I missed sailing. One day when I was looking for our ad in *Sail,* I noticed an announcement for a singlehanded sailboat race. The race was designed to retrace the route of the legendary clipper ships of the nineteenth century from New York to San Francisco by way of Cape Horn. I was interested and sent away for a prospectus.

The race was sponsored by the Expedition Marketing Group and endorsed by the Society of Lone Offshore Sailors (SOLOS). It was a nonstop event, open to qualified sailors in boats up to 45 feet long. They deliberately discouraged maxi-boats and maxi-type expenses. The starting date was October 15, 1982. If I wanted to enter, I had six months to finagle a boat, find a sponsor, convince Tom that my participation in the race would be a public relations windfall for the school, and sell Molly on the idea.

The last part was the easiest. Molly thought the race was an exciting idea, and she became my chief supporter. Tom knew as well as I did that it was not PR for the school that was motivating me, but he also thought I should enter. He and Molly both volunteered to take up my duties and keep the school running in my absence. I've been incredibly blessed to have a supportive family for all of my farfetched schemes.

The more I thought about the race, the more I wanted to be a part of it. Cape Horn. The mere thought of the rocky island at the tip of South America sent shivers down my spine. It terrified me and it challenged me. Somehow it called out to me. But was I qualified to even consider a windward passage around Cape Horn, surely one of the most demanding passages on the planet? Mountaineers dream of Everest and sailors dream of the Horn. On paper I wasn't even close to qualified. I'd only singlehanded a couple of times, and I'd never been within ten thousand miles of the infamous Southern Ocean. But was I qualified in my heart? I didn't know, but I had to find out. I mailed in the entry form.

Epoch was not the right boat for a 16,000-mile slug to windward. She tracked poorly, and other aspects of her design worried me. Her large cockpit was vulnerable to being swamped, and her rig was difficult to manage alone. Also, she was in desperate need of a complete refitting. I needed a rugged boat, one expressly designed for solo sailing.

Tom suggested I call our good friend Bob Cheadle in Toronto. Bob was the marketing manager for Contessa Yachts of Canada, and had referred many students to The Navigation School. Bob's company manufactured one of my favorite designs, the Contessa 32. The 32 had striking lines and a proud reputation. When I told Bob about the race, he was eager to get involved. He agreed with me, and thought that a Contessa 32, although a bit small by Cape Horn standards, was an excellent boat for singlehanded ocean racing.

Although Contessa of Toronto builds the boat on license from the British parent company, Bob urged me to sail a British-made boat. "John, the Brits understand heavy-weather sailing," Bob assured me. And coincidentally, he just happened to have a British boat available. The only problem was that it was 4,000 miles from Ft. Lauderdale, in Point Roberts, Washington.

We eventually worked out a deal, and the school agreed to lease the boat for two years. I also agreed to pay for shipping and insurance. It was an economical way for me to enter the race, and Molly and I immediately began to solicit potential equipment sponsors. I scheduled a June qualifying passage to Bermuda, and we started to compile lists of spares and provisions. Although the Contessa would be the smallest boat in the race, I honestly felt I could win.

Our preparations were charging ahead, and I'd even convinced

Hood Sails to outfit the boat when I received an urgent letter from Expedition Marketing. I tore open the envelope and read the letter. "No," I hollered. "No, they can't do this." The race had been cancelled. I was crushed.

Aside from my great personal disappointment, I had also saddled our struggling school with another unnecessary boat expense. Yet, there was nothing to do but forget about the race and get on with the business of The Navigation School. Ah, but I was destined for Cape Horn — one way or another. Although I didn't know it at the time, one of my students would be the key to a Cape Horn clipper ship race of my own.

I met Ty Techera when he enrolled in our May 1982 seminar. He flew down from Michigan just to attend the class. My initial impression of him was that, although he was a sharp student, he was a mere armchair adventurer at heart, and celestial navigation would be a hobby, not a ticket to roam the oceans. He owned a 23-foot sloop that he daysailed on Lake St. Clair. My assessment was dead wrong.

Ty remained to chat one day after class. Almost apologetically, he confided in me that he wanted to sail across the Atlantic in the fall. He had almost no experience, and I was skeptical as he detailed his plan. He wanted to take advantage of the strong U.S. dollar abroad, buy a boat in Europe, and sail her home. Ty's scheme made financial sense, but unfortunately, his knowledge of European sailboats was as limited as his sailing experience. Then I had an idea.

"Ty, the school owns a French boat and leases a British boat. The Contessa 32, the British boat, might be just the boat for you. How would you like to take her for a sail?"

"I'd love to, John, and I will buy you dinner afterwards."

"It's a deal," I answered.

The boat was just a few blocks from the school, and soon after boarding we had cleared Port Everglades and were gliding over the Gulf Stream swell. I explained how I had originally hoped to sail the boat around Cape Horn. I also told Ty about the boat's sterling performance in the 1979 Fastnet Race disaster, a disaster in which 15 lives were lost and numerous boats sunk. Every Contessa 32 in the race finished. Ty was impressed with the way the boat handled. I tried to talk him into buying the school's boat, deviously scheming to sneak out of our lease commitment, but he was determined to purchase a boat overseas.

Gin preceded dinner, two bottles of Vouvray accompanied the fish, and brandy followed. We talked about passagemaking, and I confessed to Ty that I wished I had the time to join him in his projected transatlantic voyage. Ty's enthusiasm for the venture was infectious, and when he offered to pay all my expenses, I agreed to sail with him in October, against my better judgment. We were staggeringly drunk, and despite the sincerity of our handshake late that evening, I did not expect to hear from Ty again.

Ty is that rare individual who decides to fetch a mark and does just that. Several months later, in August, he called the school. His distant voice proudly informed me that he was in Lymington, England and had just ordered a new Contessa 32. "Oh, no," I thought to myself, "the fool's gone ahead and bought a boat. Now he wants me to keep my end of the bargain." I tried to be vague on the phone. "That's great, Ty. Oh, ya, I remember . . . uh huh . . . yes . . . Well, OK, great talking to you. Goodbye."

After I hung up the phone, a multitude of questions rushed through my head. How can I afford to leave the school for two months? How can I cancel out of delivering that Morgan 46 to the Bahamas? What am I going to tell Molly?

"Who was that on the phone?" Molly asked.

"A guy named Ty Techera. Remember, I took him sailing a few months ago. He just bought a new Contessa 32 in England."

"That's neat, but what did he want?" she wondered.

"Well, baby, he wants me to help him sail across the Atlantic in November."

"He didn't just call out of the blue to ask you to sail with him, did he?"

"No," I confessed. Then I explained my drunken commitment.

Molly did not respond right away. "Well, John, you need a passage. You haven't been worth a damn ever since the race was cancelled. I'll miss you, but if you want to sail, then you should."

I realized I was fully committed to the project in early September when Ty and I flew to England to visit the Contessa factory in Lymington. *Gigi,* Ty's boat to be, named after his wife, was just a bare, fiberglass shell, patiently being constructed to Lloyds of London's 100-A1 specifications. Ty insisted on this high construction standard, and it is a bothersome procedure for a builder. A Lloyds surveyor must be present during each crucial stage of development.

We met Jeremy Rogers, the founder and backbone of Contessa Yachts and one of England's premier yachtsmen. We had many specific requests to customize the boat for offshore sailing. Jeremy felt we were wasting our money, but obliged us, thinking to himself, "these extravagant Americans." We decided to strengthen the standard deck by adding ½ inch of Airex core throughout. We also added an extra, full-length Airex stringer to the hull. In addition to stiffening the hull, the stringers helped to encapsulate the bulkheads and keep them from breaking loose in rough seas. We also increased the size of the standing rigging and opted for a cutter stay, or baby stay, on a block and tackle.

Our original plan was to depart the south coast of England in mid-October for the 1,500-mile jaunt to the Canary Islands. We hoped to miss the traditional equinoctial gales of late September and be well south before the November storms marched across the English Channel and Bay of Biscay. Unfortunately, our plans were snagged when Contessa telexed Ty in early October and announced that *Gigi* was way behind schedule and would not be ready to sail before November 7.

Ty called me at the school and presented the dilemma. He wondered if we should ship the boat to Gibraltar because of the late date. I could sense he was testing me. We had agreed that I was captain, and I had my first decision to make. I told him I would call him back. After hanging up the phone, I unrolled the November pilot chart for the North Atlantic. Our crossing was divided into two distinct passages: from England south to the Canaries, and from the Canaries on across the Atlantic. It was the first passage that concerned me.

According to the pilot chart, we could expect miserable conditions in the English Channel and Bay of Biscay. Headwinds averaging 25 to 30 knots and frequent gale possibilities. Temperatures in the forties, large seas, and fog completed the expected scenario. Yet I did not want to suggest that I was not up to the task, so I called Ty back and told him we should proceed with our original plans to depart from England.

We arrived in England on November 7, 1982, and a frantic week later *Gigi* was ready to sail. Preparing a new boat for an ocean crossing is a formidable task in your home port. In a foreign country, racing against nature's timetable, it's an especially difficult job. The afternoon before our departure I left Ty, the designated cook, to stow the provisions. I hiked into town and met with Jeremy Rogers. We had a pint of lager and talked about the infamous '79 Fastnet Race.

"What tactics did *Ascent* adopt during the height of the storm?" I quizzed Jeremy. *Ascent,* a Contessa 32, not only finished the race, she won her class.

"John, she simply kept on with the race. She didn't heave-to, run off, or lie ahull. She held her course under storm canvas and prevented knockdowns by luffing up into the largest waves. She was handled superbly, but this boat can take a lot of punishment."

November 15, 1982, departure day, was hectic from the beginning. Contessa contacted the BBC and they sent a reporter down to the boat. A correspondent from *Yachting Monthly* magazine also dropped by for a chat. Our voyage was newsworthy because of our late departure, and, I think, in the eyes of the Brits, our lack of experience. When we finally shoved off, Ty and I were inflated with our nouveau celebrity status. The English Channel had a special dose of humility waiting for us.

We cleared the Lymington River and set the main and jib in the Solent. A cold, brisk northerly wind whisked us toward the Needles Channel where we had an appointment with slack tide. Through the Needles, we were into the English Channel. Our next scheduled stop was La Palma in the Canary Islands, 1,500 miles to the south.

We had only test sailed *Gigi* once before our departure. For six hours the sailing was exhilarating, but fish-scale clouds foretold a change in the weather. The barren headland of Portland Bill was obscured as the sky turned gray and the wind began to back to the west. An hour later the wind veered to the southwest and piped up to 35 knots. We were hard on the wind, and it was necessary to reef the main and shorten the roller-furling headsail. Ty had insisted on roller-furling, and I was skeptical about whether it would endure a prolonged blow.

When it began to rain, my spirits plummeted. Suddenly I felt nervous and overwhelmed with responsibility. I wanted Molly aboard. *Gigi* was easy handling in the strong winds and choppy seas, but I worried about Ty's inexperience. He was, for the first time, sailing beyond the reassuring sight of land. I tried to steady myself, telling myself that I had a job to do, to sail *Gigi* across the Atlantic to America, but America seemed about a million miles away. In a phrase, I was frightened, not of the gale, but of my responsibility.

Ty, on the other hand, was managing beautifully. I had prepped him for the possibility of nasty weather, and because we seemed to be handling the situation, he wondered what I was worried about. Experience is multifaceted, and Ty, a novice sailor, used the wisdom of an old sea dog to cheer up his young captain. He gave me an inspirational pep talk and assured me that he had complete confidence in me. Then, despite the gale-force conditions, he went below and concocted a welcome hot meal. My mood brightened as I sipped a steaming cup of tea. Although we didn't know it then, we were in for a brutal week. Through every gale we battled, it was my experience and Ty's enthusiasm which kept us on track.

Our westward progress slowed dramatically as we pounded into confused, steep seas. We bashed to windward in a series of four-hour tacks, and for 36 hours we crisscrossed the Channel. The weather was not our only concern — the amount of commercial shipping in the English Channel is appalling. Several times we altered our course to avoid a freighter, and, in the process, lost hours of hard-fought westing in a matter of minutes. I obtained two reliable RDF bearings on the night of November 16, and plotted a fix. The result was disheartening; in a day and a half of hard sailing, we'd managed to claw our way just 50 miles to the west.

Ty and I were exhausted, cold, and soaked to the core. *Gigi* has only 28 inches of freeboard, and although she is a splendid, seakindly boat, she is wet. Indeed, the Brits call the Contessa 32 a submarine with sails. We needed a break. I quickly studied the chart and decided Dartmouth, just north of Start Point, was the nearest all-weather harbor along the south coast. We jibed over and sailed due north. Cautiously, we sounded our way into the harbor around midnight. We tied up at the Yacht Haven Marina and collapsed into our berths. We hoped to sneak out of the marina early the next morning, but we were unable. It seemed as though everyone at the marina had heard the BBC broadcast and wanted to help us. We were delayed a day, but had time to make a few quick repairs and dry out our clothes.

The weather forecast called for a gradual clearing as we motored out of Dartmouth Harbor. Our confidence had been rejuvenated by the brief respite. The weather was still cloudy and blustery, but we felt we'd seen the worst of it.

Six hours out of Dartmouth a huge low-pressure system developed, and we were in the midst of a Force 8 gale: 35- to 40-knot winds and 10-foot seas. The gale blew out of the southwest, and once again we were forced to beat into it. All day and into the night we tacked into the teeth of the storm. At 0200 on November 19, 1982, the rain turned to sleet and the wind increased to a steady 45 knots. It was futile to press on; we were making little headway. Instead, we tied in the third reef and set the staysail on the cutter stay and hove-to. *Gigi* rode 60 degrees off the wind, and we kept our eyes peeled for freighters. We lay hove-to until daybreak. We were greeted by a gray dawn and a foreboding forecast which predicted that the storm would last another day. Visibility was dreadful, and I decided prudence dictated seeking shelter along the coast.

I let the backwinded staysail go and pulled it around. We hardened the sheets and set the course for Plymouth. We ran toward the English coast with the wind on the port quarter, and I had a disturbing hunch that we had not made much westward progress. Visibility improved, and just before nightfall the dark outline of the coast came into view. I strained my eyes to identify the headland off the bow. I missed Molly's eyes. It wasn't, it couldn't be, it was. Start Point again, and dead ahead. In another day and a half of rugged, windward sailing, we had not

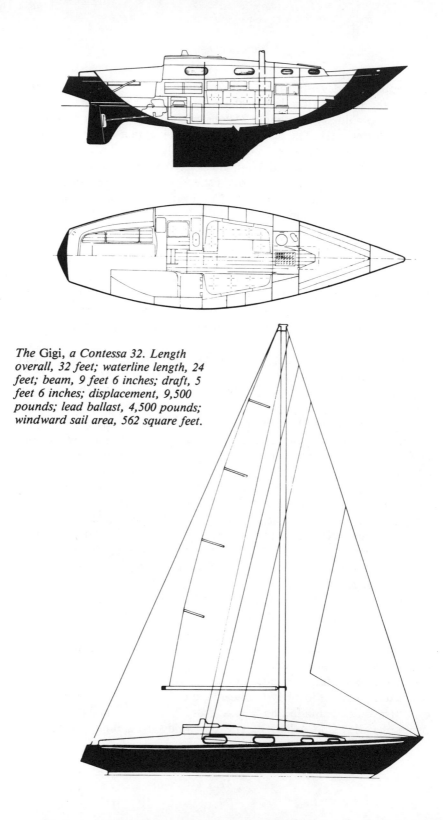

The Gigi, *a Contessa 32. Length overall, 32 feet; waterline length, 24 feet; beam, 9 feet 6 inches; draft, 5 feet 6 inches; displacement, 9,500 pounds; lead ballast, 4,500 pounds; windward sail area, 562 square feet.*

inched our way one mile farther west. Would we ever get out of the Channel?

Reluctantly, we abandoned hopes of making Plymouth and decided to return to Dartmouth again — at least we knew the way into the harbor. The black of a moonless night descended upon us, and the wind really began to howl. The wind-speed indicator registered several gusts at the top of the scale — 54 knots. I was apprehensive about approaching the coast too quickly and decided to lower the main and staysail to slow our speed to 5 knots. As Start Point light cast its eerie reflection upon the water every 10 seconds, we could see the frightening heights of the waves silhouetted against the light.

Then, without warning, a steeply curled, black wave unleashed its fury over the transom. Water rushed over the length of the boat and swamped the cockpit. *Gigi* heeled 60 degrees to starboard and then to port, but she kept her feet. Ty and I were flung about the cockpit and thankful for the short tethers on our safety harnesses. Even though the companionway boards were in place, a foot of water flooded above the cabin sole. The boat rolled sluggishly with so much water in her and was vulnerable to being pooped again. I scrambled to the foredeck and set the staysail for steerage way. It had been a mistake to ride under bare poles: When would I learn my lesson? Ty bailed frantically and I steered for the lee of Start Point. The windchill factor was in the twenties when we tied *Gigi* up at the same slip we had left 40 hours before. We were not heroes or even a novelty this time around; we were cold, frustrated, and thoroughly humbled sailors. We pumped *Gigi* dry, secured her docklines, and checked into a hotel.

The following day, and another miserable one at that, we avoided the marina as we crept around the quaint old village of Dartmouth. We spent most of November 20, 1983, drowning our sorrows in English bitters. In the drafty King's Head Pub we pondered our alternatives. Unless we wanted to leave the boat and wait for spring, or admit defeat and put her on a truck on the Continent, or ship the damn thing across the Atlantic on a freighter, we had to get going. With each passing day the wintery weather was closer to settling in. Ty ordered another round of beer, and I considered skipping ship and taking up residence in Dartmouth. November 21 dawned clear and cool, and by midday we had cleared Dartmouth harbor for the last time.

We devised a risky alternative strategy. We decided to make shorter tacks and hug the coast. If the weather changed rapidly, we could quickly head for cover and avoid losing hard-fought westing. This strategy defied my basic instincts, but our need to make westerly progress was paramount. There were many safe harbors we could duck into along the way. We managed 130 miles before we dodged a forecast gale and called into Falmouth Harbor.

Just after noon on November 24, 1982, we stoically watched Falmouth Light, at St. Anthony's Head, slowly dip below the horizon. *Gigi* relished the lee afforded by Lizard Point, but our respite from the elements would be temporary according to the BBC. "For the area of Sole, Fastnet, and Biscay (our intended sailing route), winds west to southwest, Force 7 (28 to 34 knots), becoming gale Force 8 (35-40) later, possibly gusting to severe gale Force 9 (41-46) locally, then Force 6 (22-27) later, local calms possible. Rain mixed with sleet, possible snow showers, then clearing later, locally some partial sun." That was a six-hour forecast!

With proper grit and a cavalier disregard for the atrocious atmospheric conditions, we sailed beyond the lee and stood out into the Channel. It was raining and soon we were soaked beneath our foul-weather gear. Yet the wind was more from the west than south, and we were able to steer our desired course for the first time in nine days. What a difference it makes to head in the direction in which you want to travel.

Gripping *Gigi*'s tiller, I conned her to windward. I delayed setting the Navik self-steering wind vane. It was actually a pleasure to steer, despite the weather. A low, foggy, scud moved in and obscured Lizard Point and our last glimpse of the English coastline. All through the night the west wind held. In the morning I actually spotted the sun briefly, and alertly snatched a couple of sextant sights. I then took an RDF bearing and crossed the LOPs. Amazingly, we were finally out of the English Channel and into the Bay of Biscay.

There was no time to celebrate, because the same old signals that foretold another brewing southwest gale soon appeared. Fish-scale clouds, a falling barometer, and a rising wind warned us to prepare *Gigi* for yet another blow. The ensuing gale was the fiercest one we'd yet encountered. The wind shifted abruptly to the south as the gale overtook us in the afternoon. Our wind-speed indicator was frequently pegged at the top of the scale. It was difficult to stand up in the cockpit, and I was thankful I didn't have to work the foredeck. The roller-furling system had functioned flawlessly through a week of almost constant gale-force winds.

We steered a westerly course to avoid being set into the Bay of Biscay by strong local currents. We clung tenaciously to our sea room. Although it is nearly impossible to accurately judge wind speed and wave heights from the pitching deck of a small sailboat, the BBC later confirmed the gale as a Force 10 (48-54 knots) storm.

The barometer started to rise drastically before dusk as the storm reached its height. But the worst was quickly over, and by midnight the tempest had nearly abated, leaving behind just a pleasant sailing breeze and a miserable swell. Exhausted (Ty and I had stood one-hour watches all day long) but cheerful, we steered 220° true, the course for the Canary Islands, which, for the first time in more than a week, I believed we might actually fetch. We also shook out the reefs in the sails for the first time since we had left Lymington 10 days before. Indeed, *Gigi* had endured a stormy christening.

4

An Expedition Formed

*A*FTER OUR STORMY ORDEAL in the English Channel and a vicious introduction to the Bay of Biscay, our fortunes improved rapidly. A stationary high-pressure system ushered in unseasonably warm weather, and we needed just four days to angle across the rest of the Bay.

We skirted Cape Finisterre, the northwest tip of Spain, and then steered south, paralleling the Iberian Peninsula. Ty was a physical wreck. His remarkable spirit was intact, but he had not slept in a week, and that takes the wind out of anyone's sails. We decided to call at Lisbon, Portugal. It was not much out of the way, and we were already so far behind our original time schedule that one more delay mattered little.

"We are not sailing one inch farther tonight, Ty. We're going to heave-to right here, and that's final."

"Come on, John, don't be so damn cautious. Let's just creep a bit closer to the coast tonight. I don't want to spend all day tomorrow making port."

"I'm sorry, Ty," I said, as I swung the tiller over and backwinded the jib.

"Why are you so goddamned sure we are where you think we are? I mean, Lisbon is supposed to be a pretty large city, and I don't see any lights up there . . .''

"Shut up, Ty, goddamnit, just shut up. You are exhausted. You have not slept in a week, so don't question my navigation. I'll take first watch. Good night."

That was final. We hove-to 20 miles offshore, between Cape Roca and Cape Rasco.

On December 1, 1982, we closed the coast at first light. Lisbon is an historic port city, but it is a deceiving approach from the north. The city is tucked on the southeast side of a steep headland, 15 miles inland on the Bay of Tejo. The only chart I had was scaled at 1:1,000,000, and the yellow splotch that was Lisbon was about the size of a dime. At noon skyscrapers pierced the haze at harbor's edge and boosted the confidence of a stubborn navigator and a weary crew.

A towering monument to Prince Henry the Navigator welcomes all mariners to Lisbon Harbor. We moored at the yacht club and cleared customs. My brief impressions of Lisbon were dreary ones. The city seemed lonely, almost frightened. The central city was strangely deserted, and the few residents scurrying about kept their eyes trained on their shoes. Upon the recommendation of a French yachtsman, we neglected to purchase diesel fuel, which he swore was lethal for any engine, and after just a couple of days in Lisbon, we departed for the Canary Islands.

Out at sea my perspective came into focus, and in my journal the night of December 3, I chastised myself for being so harsh on Lisbon. I wrote that I was no better than a snooty tourist who judges America after a visit to Disney World.

The wind was light, and our progress was slow as we ran our diesel only begrudgingly. Two days out of Lisbon, *Gigi* lay becalmed on a placid ocean, and Ty and I were below eating breakfast. We were aroused by a sudden rumble and dashed into the cockpit to watch horrified as a small tramp freighter steamed by just 50 yards astern. Obviously, no one was on the bridge and the ship was on autopilot. If the ship's course had been one degree more to the south, it would have crushed *Gigi*. We decided to keep a pair of eyes in the cockpit at all times.

On December 5, 1982, as *Gigi* eased along in gentle Force 3 conditions, I spotted a bottle off the starboard beam. I quickly jibed about, and on the second pass Ty scooped it aboard. Sure enough, there was a message inside. Eagerly, Ty pried the cork out. Was it a note from a sailor in distress? How far had it traveled? Had it drifted to us from a distant corner of the globe? Ty removed the note from within with the needle-nose pliers. Carefully, he unrolled it. It was a printed form from the cruise ship *Black Prince*. It had three printed lines for name, address, and country. It was probably one of a thousand dropped over the side. What a disappointment. By the way, if Michael Berg of Den Haig, Netherlands is reading, we found your note. On the back of the message it stated that it had been dropped 350 miles west of Gibraltar. We scooped it up at 32° 30′ N, 14° 40′ W. The bottle had drifted the staggering distance of about 150 miles.

There is nowhere to hide in a small boat on a placid ocean. There is very little in the way of shipboard activity, and you must confront your thoughts head-on. My thoughts were mostly about Molly. I missed her. I craved to hold her body next to mine and I longed to talk to her. We had a single-sideband radio, but we had not figured out how to use it yet. I resorted to my journal instead. On December 6, I wrote:

> *"We're becalmed, baby, in the horse latitudes. Rumor has it they used to slaughter horses to feed the crew, hence the name. I pity those poor animals. Forty-eight hours with little or no wind. Oh, baby, I miss you. Loneliness and a feeling of helplessness are driving me crazy. I can't stand to let this time pass without sharing it with you. Why did you ever let me talk you into letting me take this trip? I navigate, I change the sails, I fix what's broken. And I think of you, constantly. I love you, Molly. We were meant to sail together, or not at all."*

Ironically, we ran out of daylight 20 miles short of La Palma, the westernmost of the Canary Islands. We were forced to heave-to for six hours during the night before we fetched the harbor at Santa Cruz the next morning. We arrived on December 8, 1982, eight days out of Lisbon.

We were eager to press on across the Atlantic, and we completed our final preparations in just three days. On December 12, we commenced our transatlantic run. A strong northeast tradewind quickly hurled *Gigi* into the broad Atlantic, and by nightfall the towering, 8,000-foot summit of Pico de los Muchachos was out of view. We were bound for Antigua in the West Indies, 2,600 miles away.

On December 13 I wrote in my journal, which was evolving into a continuing love letter:

> *"This is the big one, babe, as Buckley says. I am winging my way toward your waiting arms at 6.5 knots. I am driving this boat hard, damn hard, and I should probably shorten sail. The thought of being 150 miles closer to you at noon tomorrow is overpowering, though. Blow winds, yippee, 25 knots, blow, blow, blow."*

The trade winds blew and blew.

The passage west from the Canary Islands to the West Indies is surely one of the loveliest sails on the planet. The tradewinds, nicknamed the ladies' trades, are generally steady and seldom reach gale force. I was hoping that once *Gigi* dipped below the 20th parallel she would average 120 miles per day by maintaining an average speed of 5 knots. Our objective was to sight Antigua in 22 days — high hopes indeed.

Although the pilot chart predicts Force 4 conditions (11-16 knot winds) over most of the route, during the first week of our passage the winds never dipped below 20 knots or rose above 30. It was great sailing. The wind was either dead astern, or (preferably) over the starboard quarter. We flew our 150 percent genoa boomed out. At week's end I was delighted to tally up 931 miles, which corresponded to a daily average of 133 miles and an hourly average of 5.5 knots.

Ty and I settled into an efficient routine of four-hour watches during the evening (always rotating double-watch nights) and an informal watch system during the day. Our only daytime rule was that somebody had to be in the cockpit. At night we each wore a safety harness.

Ty was the cook and cook he did. He served up heaping portions of stews, pastas, and soups. I was amazed at how he could happily spend a couple of hours every afternoon fussing over lunch. He was equally amazed at how much of his concoctions I could devour and how quickly.

Ty took to the sea naturally. He was never seasick, never flustered or frightened (sometimes a bit pushy), and always eager to learn the tricks of seamanship. Once he mastered sleeping in four-hour intervals, he was at ease in our watery environ. In short, he was a good companion.

Our second week at sea was nearly a replay of our first. We reeled off 935 miles. *Gigi* was screaming across the ocean. Cumulus clouds framed by brilliant patches of blue sky; sparkling, rolling, following seas; and warm, tropical temperatures accompanied the steady northeast tradewinds. After two weeks we were only 700 miles east of Antigua.

A successful offshore passage is usually the result of proper preparation and first-class equipment. *Gigi*'s self-steering wind vane is a fine example. She was fitted with a French-built Navik. The Navik vane is lightweight, but both durable and reliable. Day after day, the Navik did the lion's share of the helmsmanship as she flawlessly steered *Gigi* before the wind. A reliable method of self-steering is fundamental for shorthanded passagemaking.

Ty had also equipped *Gigi* with a single-sideband radio. I initially thought the SSB was a waste of $4,000, an expensive gadget that would never survive the hostile, corrosive sea environment. Theoretically, we could place calls to the U.S. from a couple of thousand miles out at sea, but I did not really believe it. The Stephens radio endured a brutal battering in the English Channel, and, to my surprise, once we figured out how to operate it, it was a pleasure to have aboard. It certainly made Christmas at sea a lot less lonely.

The barometer started to fall the day after Christmas, and I had a disturbing hunch that the Atlantic was not going to let us slip completely across her outer edge without a fight. The atmospheric pressure kept plunging throughout the 27th and 28th of December. Gradually, blue skies gave way to gray, overcast conditions, and the steady tradewinds piped up to gale force.

Gigi charged down the faces of huge following seas on December 30. It was impossible to obtain sextant sights through the thick overcast. After 2,500 miles, we were forced to approach Antigua under dead reckoning. At 1800 on December 31, 1982, I reckoned we were just 40 miles east of Antigua. The winds increased to a steady 35 knots, and the reefs guarding Antigua's eastern coastline presented a dangerous lee shore. It was painfully obvious that if we continued on we would arrive in the middle of the night — again. I decided to heave-to while we still had plenty of sea room, and let the powerful rollers slowly ease us toward the island. Ty agreed wholeheartedly with me.

A rare Force 9 (40-46 knots) Caribbean gale developed during the night. I worried about our leeway. Although we were hove-to, we were definitely drifting toward land faster than I wanted. I peered at the dark horizon toward the east and strained my ears for the distant sound of breaking surf. A very welcome dawn only confused us more. We could not see Antigua, or any of the other Leeward Islands for that matter. Where were the West Indies?

The wind subsided a bit during the morning, and the sun shone briefly from behind a cloud. I snatched a sight and quickly plotted a longitude line of position. According to the sight, we were on the meridian of St. Johns, Antigua. Where in hell was the island? Something was wrong.

"Hey, there it is," Ty shouted excitedly.

"Where?" I questioned, as I looked in the direction he pointed toward, off the bow.

"There, above the clouds. We're almost on top of the damn island."

Ty was right. The lush, green mountainside of the island was clearly visible above the cloud layer. We had crossed the Atlantic. It was January 1, 1983. *Gigi* had completed the run in just over 19 days by averaging 134 miles per day. To put that in perspective, consider it this way: *Gigi*'s hull speed is 6.6 knots; we averaged 5.6 knots, or 85 percent of hull speed for 19 consecutive days.

We rapidly approached the island, and I dug out our harbor chart of Antigua. We wanted to drop anchor in English Harbor on the southeast side of the island. As we neared the coast and entered the lee, we lowered our sails for the first time in nearly three weeks, and continued under power. I could not seem to match the island's topographical features with those on the chart. We motored almost completely around the island, but we couldn't find English Harbor. I was desperate, so we approached a fishing skiff for advice.

"Hey, which way to English Harbor?" I called out.

"No, no, mon. This is Montserrat, mon. English Harbor is on Antigua about 20 miles northeast."

Ty and I looked at each other, and he smiled broadly. "Go ahead," I said, "give it to me. I deserve it. Question my goddamned navigation." I was laughing and so was Ty.

"I don't care what fucking island this is," he said. "Let's anchor and get the hell off the boat."

We anchored in Old Road Bay on the west side of Montserrat and immediately rowed ashore. We staggered up a steep hill toward the bar with the firm ground swaying beneath our unsteady feet. The ground swayed even more on the way down the hill, but I don't think it was land-sickness. Early the next morning we pulled up the anchor and beat over to English Harbor.

I called Molly. She was thrilled to hear from me, but she had some disturbing news. The Navigation School was on the verge of bankruptcy. She had intentionally neglected to tell me when I called at Christmas, because she did not want to burden me with it while I was at sea. Molly understands sailing. She told me that she had to cancel several classes because of lack of interest. We decided to go ahead with our plans to exhibit at the New York National Boat Show in a week, and I told her I would fly home immediately.

I was leaving Ty in the lurch; his boat was still 1,500 miles from Florida where he planned to berth it for the winter. I pleaded with him to take a crewman along with him, but he wouldn't hear of it. He also insisted I return to the mainland as soon as possible, and he bought my ticket. He viewed singlehanding to Florida as the culmination of his learning process, the final test of his apprenticeship. I felt miserable as I boarded the plane. I dreaded the impending financial crisis at the school, and I hated leaving Ty. At least Molly would be home waiting for me.

I returned to Florida on January 4, 1983, and Ty left English Harbor the next day alone. He arrived in Miami 12 days later. He handled a gale, mastered celestial navigation, and overcame intense loneliness. His voyage was a great success until he overslept on his approach to Miami and nearly piled up on the beach. He had been sleeping in 15-minute intervals when his wristwatch alarm failed to rouse him. Miraculously, he awoke just in time to save *Gigi*. The boat was only 100 yards off the beach before he slammed the tiller over and jibed about.

Molly and I loaded the car with signs, banners, and boxes of brochures. We arrived in New York City on January 10, 1983, and set up our booth at the Coliseum on 58th Street. We desperately needed to fill two Manhattan seminars, scheduled for February, to keep the school afloat.

Over a million people filtered through the maze of boats and accessories at the New York National Boat Show. The show was a great success, and we registered 12 students for both the celestial and coastal navigation seminars; 24 students times $300 tuition equals $7,200 gross!

I returned to Manhattan in February to conduct the classes, and I was already scheming how we would use the money to promote other seminars. On the night of the first class, the city was paralyzed by the worst snowstorm of the century. The blizzard raged for three straight days and the entire town was shut down. Needless to say, the classes were a financial disaster. I was obligated to return most of the deposits I'd collected, and when I returned to Ft. Lauderdale we decided to close the school. We cancelled all of our leases and liquidated most of our assets. For a year and a half we'd worked furiously to make the school a success, but on March 1, 1983, we had very little to show for our efforts. We had enough money to live on for several months, and, luckily, promptly arranged a couple of yacht deliveries, which enhanced our reserves.

My mom was still determined to sail around the world. She had befriended Captain Tim MacTaggart, a down-on-his-luck charterboat captain, who shared her dream. They hit it off immediately and decided to refit the *Epoch* and make sail for distant horizons together. It was tough to turn the *Epoch* over to Mom and Tim. One epoch was ending, but another was just beginning.

In April, Ty asked us to deliver *Gigi* north to Detroit, her port on the Great Lakes. For the 1,000-mile dash up the coast, a former student, Bill Oswald from Houston, joined Molly and me. Oz (as he's known to all), an experienced small-boat racing sailor, had recently purchased a 42-foot ketch and was anxious to gain bluewater experience.

Gigi sprinted up the coast. Propelled by a sprawling, lightweight spinnaker and assisted by the generous Gulf Stream current, we averaged

166 miles per day. We arrived in New York on May 2, 1983, completing a six-day passage. Oz skipped ship in New York and Molly and I continued on. Our route to Detroit led us up the Hudson River to Albany, through the Erie Barge Canal, and across Lake Ontario and Lake Erie. We sailed up the Detroit River and into Lake St. Clair on May 23. Late that afternoon, I eased *Gigi* into her slip on the Clinton River in Mt. Clemens, Michigan. For the time being, anyway, her travels were over, and, unfortunately, so were ours.

We had come full circle; we were back where we had begun three and a half years before. We moved into Mom's empty house in the suburbs and felt like miserable misfits. Molly took a job in a dog kennel, and I started to write, but did not finish, a couple of sailing articles. I was despondent. I felt as if I'd plunged into the depths of Tartarus, stranded in Michigan, 700 miles from the ocean.

Ty and I spent many summer afternoons sailing on Lake St. Clair. One hazy afternoon in July we let *Gigi* bob aimlessly on the placid lake while we took to swatting flies and drinking our 12-pack of beer.

"So, what do you do next?" Ty inquired.

"I don't know. I guess I'll line up a delivery south in the fall and take it from there." I wasn't very enthusiastic. I knew I had to promote some kind of sailing endeavor promptly, or I was faced with the dreary prospect of having to find a job. Sipping a beer, I pondered Ty's question. What would I do next?

A collage of memories and dreams raced through my mind. I pictured myself on a screaming reach, recklessly charging for the Golden Gate Bridge, the finishing mark for the cancelled Cape Horn Clipper Ship race. I remembered shipping *Jeanne* to Florida when I had been a bungling but ambitious landlubber; the peaceful anchorages in the Caribbean; the jungles of Costa Rica; the gales of the English Channel . . . .

"Why don't you go to work for me at the plant?" Ty said, interrupting my daydreaming. "I'll pay you well, and in a year or two you will have enough money to buy another boat."

"Ugh," I thought to myself. "How about another beer?" Avoiding Ty's offer of employment, I gulped down the beer and dove over the side. The water was soberingly cold. I swam a considerable distance from the boat before I turned back and admired her lines. Like me, *Gigi* seemed out of her element in Michigan. She was designed, constructed, and equipped for offshore sailing. As I struggled to tread water, a devious thought, a wonderfully devious thought, came to mind. I didn't need an official race to sail around Cape Horn. The true race was with

Gigi, at 32 feet, compared to a fully rigged clipper, 229 feet overall. Drawing done to scale.

history and the legendary clipper ships of the 1850s. *Gigi* was the perfect boat for a race of my own!

I vigorously swam back to the boat and climbed aboard. "Ty, my friend, I have a proposition for you," I announced brazenly.

"OK, let's hear it."

"Ty, we should sail *Gigi* in the wake of the mighty clipper ships, retracing their route from New York to San Francisco by way of Cape Horn."

Ty had downed a few more beers while I was swimming, and at first he was confused. He cocked his head, gazed off toward Canada, and considered my crazy proposition. "Well," he said after a couple of minutes, "that's the best idea you've ever had. When can we leave?"

"Yahoo," I shouted. I was back in business.

The sun dipped below the horizon and the northern twilight lingered as the first details of our audacious sailing journey took shape.

My hangover the next morning did not dim the enthusiasm of the previous night's commitment. I immediately launched our preparations for the 16,000-mile voyage. I decided to stage an imaginary race by attempting to complete the voyage in a time comparable to an 1850s clipper ship.

The evolution of commercial sailing ships reached its zenith with the development of the towering clippers. A bark-rigged clipper ship was usually well over 200 feet long, radically lean and fine entried. Clippers dominated a brief but glorious age of sail.

Industrious Yankee shipbuilders constructed clipper ships for two reasons — speed and profit — and the two were interchangeable. Originally, clipper ship masters catered to a young nation's thirst for fresh tea from the Orient, and were not above padding their profits by stashing a bit of opium in the hold. But it was the discovery of gold in California in 1849 that caused the clipper ships to dominate travel on the high seas.

Before the completion of the transcontinental railroad, and long before the opening of the Panama Canal, clipper ships and the daring men who sailed them conquered the challenge of the American continent. The fastest way from any East Coast port to the gold fields was on the wings of a swift clipper ship. Thousands of greedy sailors braved the brutal passage to San Francisco.

San Francisco sprang up almost overnight during the gold-rush days. It was a wild boom town, and products from back East sold at incredibly inflated prices. Clippers carried finished products as well as gold miners, and the fastest ships charged the highest freights. Competition was intense. Zealous captains carried canvas long after prudence dictated reefing, and, if their ships held together, they accomplished remarkable passages. By the early 1850s, the average passage time between New York and San Francisco had been whittled down to 120 days. However, the swiftest ship of all, *Flying Cloud,* twice completed the long voyage in just 89 days, a record still unbeaten under sail. I decided 120 sailing days would be *Gigi*'s objective.

Because of *Gigi*'s diminutive stature and logistical problems, it wasn't practical for us to sail nonstop as the clippers had done. I divided the voyage into four passages: the shakedown, New York to Bermuda (700 miles); Leg I, Bermuda to Rio de Janeiro, Brazil (4,500 miles); Leg II, Rio de Janeiro to Valparaiso, Chile (4,200 miles); and Leg III, Valparaiso to San Francisco (5,600 miles).

More than just the ghosts of clipper ship captains inspired me. The call of Cape Horn, the tip of the American continent, lured me like a magnet. My research turned up some interesting data. *Gigi* would become the smallest American yacht, and one of only a handful of yachts, to ever double Cape Horn the hard way, from east to west, against the prevailing winds and currents. Specifically, doubling the Horn means to sail direct from 50°S in the Atlantic Ocean, around the Horn, and up to 50°S in the Pacific. An old clipper ship chantey described the rugged loop:

> *"From fifty south to fifty south*
> *You won't grow fat and lazy*
> *For the winds that howl around Cape Horn*
> *Will surely drive you crazy."*

According to the Boat U.S. Research Foundation, *Gigi* would be the first yacht to retrace the entire route from New York to San Francisco.

Molly was not excited about the expedition. She was willing to spend a few years land-based, working and saving to buy our own boat. She did not suffer from acute Cape Horn fever as I did. She longed for tranquil lagoons in the South Pacific and a steady tradewind over the starboard quarter. Selfishly, I argued that this was an opportunity of a lifetime, and she just had to be part of the expedition. It was a difficult period for us because, without really consulting her, I had committed all our funds and at least a year of my time to the project. I can get carried away about offshore sailing. It's more than an avocation or even a vocation for me; it's a passion. We finally reached a compromise. Molly agreed to help me deliver *Gigi* back to New York and accompany me on the shakedown and Leg I.

Sea trials on Lake St. Clair, Michigan.

Ty, much to his dismay, could not find the time to sail the entire 16,000 miles. Instead, he signed on for the shakedown to Bermuda and Leg II, the Cape Horn run. For the third leg, the longest of the voyage, I contacted Oz in Houston. He was excited about joining our team and agreed to crew on the home stretch. I was designated the captain, and planned to sail from start to finish. By the middle of August, my motley lot of crewmembers were all committed to the voyage. We had one month before we planned to leave Detroit and what seemed like a year's worth of work ahead of us.

Preparing for an extended offshore journey can be more trying than executing it. Although *Gigi* was already superbly equipped, much of her gear was worn. To conquer Cape Horn, *Gigi* had to be shipshape. The costs of our preparations were staggering. We hauled the boat, painted the bottom, and changed the sacrificial zincs. We overhauled the diesel and sorted out a few electrical problems. We restocked the spare parts inventory and purchased charts and provisions. It's amazing how the costs add up. Ty decided to replace every deck fitting and shackle on board, as well as the running rigging.

Our financial burden was eased when Ty persuaded the Stroh Brewery Co., of Detroit, to sponsor us. Stroh's commissioned North Sails of Mt. Clemens to custom design and build two heavy-weather sails. The sails, a 7-ounce mainsail and a 10-ounce, two-ply 105 percent jib, were decorated with the colorful trademark of Stroh's super premium beer, Signature.

We glided down the Detroit River on September 15, 1983, bound for New York. Although we still had many loose ends to tie, basically I felt that *Gigi* was ready for the challenging task ahead. As we cleared the river and sailed into Lake Erie, my stomach was churning with anticipation. We were embarking on a voyage I'd been dreaming about for years. It was a daunting prospect, and I wondered if I was capable of it. My stomach was churning a bit too much, and the intrepid captain was miserably seasick on the first day of the voyage.

A cold west wind drove *Gigi* across Lake Erie, and I eventually found my sea legs. A hearty Canadian chap braved a driving rainstorm and helped secure our lines at the Port Colburn Marina on the northeast end of the lake. Trying to regain a bit of self-esteem, rather boastfully I told him that we were ultimately bound for San Francisco by way of Cape Horn. He assured me that with Lake Erie behind us the hard part was over.

Molly and I proceeded to cross Lake Ontario and traverse the 38 locks of the Erie Barge Canal. We powered down the Hudson River. We circled Manhattan Island and worked our way up the East River, carefully timing our passage through Hell Gate with the flood tide. We passed beneath Throgs Neck Bridge and entered Long Island Sound. *Gigi* skirted the yachts moored off City Island before we finally tucked behind Davenport Neck and tied up at the Harbor View Marina in New Rochelle. We had one week before our scheduled departure.

5

A False Start

*T*HE FINAL WEEK ASHORE before an extended offshore passage is chaotic. Oz and Ty joined Molly and me, and we worked frantically. Once the mast was standing again, we assembled and installed a new roller-furling system, carefully inspected the standing rigging, serviced the seacocks, and provisioned. Gradually, we placed a check mark next to most of the "must-do" items on our four-page master project list.

Gigi looked like a toy rafted alongside my friend Edd Kalehoff's 52-foot classic yawl, *Magic Venture.* In fact, some snide onlookers suggested that we were loading the wrong boat. Another friend, John Evans, who lives aboard his cutter, *Victoria,* took a keen interest in our voyage. John is a Welshman of surprising versatility. He has sailed the Atlantic a dozen times as a delivery skipper, but when he finally washed ashore in New York, he changed tacks. He went into publishing and today he is the publisher of the *Village Voice.* Yet, I could sense that his anchor ashore was starting to drag. When we spent an evening in *Victoria*'s roomy cabin talking of Cape Horn and beyond, I could see the glint in his eyes; the sea was beckoning.

John helped us track down hard-to-find items and arranged to write

Ty Techera and Molly Potter.

a series of progress reports for *Sail* magazine. I also conned him into using *Victoria* as our press boat on departure day.

I took time out from our hectic schedule to contact officials at the South Street Seaport Museum in New York. I hoped that we could tie up at the Seaport briefly the day before we left and conduct a press conference. The museum not only refused us permission to tie up, they scorned our voyage. It turned out that they were endorsing Chay Blythe, who, aboard his 65-foot trimaran *Beefeater,* was also planning to sail from New York to San Francisco. Blythe's objective was to break *Flying Cloud*'s long-standing record of 89 days. It was the first I had heard of his attempt, and, although I have nothing against Blythe personally (indeed, he is a highly accomplished sailor), I did find it galling that the museum was supporting a Briton's attempt to beat a very American record. (Unfortunately, *Beefeater* never made it to the starting line. She was abandoned by her delivery crew east of New York when one of her outer pontoons was holed. I recently learned — November 1984 — that Chay is having another go at it, and recently left New York. Although he publicly tried to discount our voyage, I still wish him fair winds; he'll need them too.)

When Molly wrapped the last package of noodles with two Zip-Loc

Gigi charging down the East River on October 15, 1983. The first day of a long journey. (Pamela Duffy photograph)

plastic bags late on the night of October 13, we declared ourselves ready. Every nook and cranny in *Gigi*'s tiny cabin was bulging with gear, and she was riding a few inches below her waterline. Early on October 14, I shook hands with Oz, and he said, "I'll see you in Chile in a couple of months, captain. Good luck." Neither one of us could have imagined then the ordeal *Gigi* would endure before she reached Chile. We followed *Victoria* across the western end of Long Island Sound and up the East River to 23rd Street Marina, where we had rescheduled our press conference.

The press came and went; *Gigi*'s voyage was news today and forgotten tomorrow. I met with the editors of *Yacht Racing and Cruising* magazine and agreed to write a series of full-length articles comparing progress with our clipper ship rivals.

Departure day, October 15, 1983, dawned clear and cool, and I was up before the sun. I crept quietly out of the boat and scaled a breakwall where I had an unobstructed view of *Gigi*. Looking down at her was like looking into a dream, surely the biggest dream of my young life. *Gigi* was chomping at the bit; we simply had to cast off her docklines and she was ready to carry us south, toward Cape Horn. An excited chill came over me, and I leaped off the wall and hastily woke the crew.

"Come on, Molly. Get up, Ty. It's time to go."

We hoisted our bright red Stroh's jib and our new, heavy-duty mainsail, which was confidently embroidered, "Cape Horn 270°." (By steering a compass course of 270° while rounding the Horn, you must leave it to starboard.) Defiantly, we passed close astern of the huge bark, *Peking,* one of the last, great Cape Horn square riggers. She has been restored and is docked at South Street Seaport. John Evans skillfully handled his boat while paralleling our course. A still photographer and a video team documented our departure. We dodged the Staten Island ferry and charged past the Statue of Liberty. At the Verrazano Bridge, *Victoria* turned back. I scurried forward and hauled up the spinnaker, Ty trimmed the sheets, and Molly steered for the open ocean. Our odyssey had begun.

Gigi's cockpit is small and designed for two people. The three of us stumbled over each other as we tried to make sense of the maze of sheets and halyards sprawled about. The 700-mile shakedown passage to Bermuda was the only time we had three people aboard. Twenty-four hours out of New York, we sailed smack into a stationary high-pressure center. Unusually balmy temperatures allowed us to work on our suntans, but there was very little wind to work with. Promptly, I was forced to make a difficult decision.

Gigi's auxiliary is a dependable, 12-horsepower Yanmar diesel. We carry 20 gallons of fuel in one main tank and 10 additional gallons in plastic jugs. Our range under power is only 350 miles, if the sea is smooth. The diesel's primary function is to generate electrical current to power our instruments, radios, lights, etc. I had to decide if it was "fair" to put the engine in gear and motor for miles as well as amperage. The clippers were obviously engineless. Ty was all for motoring. He argued that 350 miles made little difference on each leg of a 16,000-mile journey. Molly, too, thought it was senseless not to use the engine. Still, I was troubled. Admittedly, the clipper ship race was merely a secondary objective; our primary goal was to raise San Francisco, one way or another, by hook or crook. I finally decided to use part of our precious fuel in light air. On subsequent legs, we burned almost every drop of fuel just charging the batteries anyway.

I hoped to complete the shakedown in less than six days, but light, annoying headwinds slowed our progress. On the fifth day out, October 20, a hard northeaster greeted us and ushered in an abrupt weather change. Driving rain and gusty winds accompanied the front. We were forced to veer to the west of the island and approach St. George, the port of entry on the east end, from the south.

During the night of October 21, the winds piped up to gale force, and powerful seas struck *Gigi* on her port quarter. The wind-speed indicator registered several gusts above 50 knots, and I couldn't help but recall our first passage to Bermuda aboard the *Epoch*. But I'd sailed thousands of miles since that first gale, and I had no intention of heaving-to or running off this time around. Besides, *Gigi* is a firm-footed stallion, and she inspires confidence in her crew.

Although I am absolutely sure that the Bermuda Triangle mystery is a myth, a few surprises turned the long night and early morning of October 22 into a nightmare.

In New York we replaced *Gigi*'s original Hood Sea Furl roller-furling system with a new, state-of-the-art unit built by Harken and North. The new furling drum looked rugged, the bearings seemed indestructible, and the aluminum extrusions that went over the forestay appeared to be first-rate. Unfortunately, the unit had a few design quirks that needed sea trials, and *Gigi* turned out to be the guinea pig. Just after midnight, with the winds steady at Force 8, the furling line chafed through at the drum. Suddenly, we went from a storm-jib-sized headsail to a 150 percent genoa! I let go the halyard in the cockpit and scrambled onto the foredeck. Ty quickly joined me. Together we could not drag the sail down to the deck. The luff was jammed in the slot on the extrusion, and we could not lower the sail. It was flogging furiously.

70

Molly, happy the voyage is underway.

Molly was also up, and she took control of the helm. I hollered for her to head up into the wind. Our only alternative was to wrap the sail around the forestay like a flag. Molly brought the bow around, and Ty and I held on for dear life as it plunged into the seas. I released the sheets and Ty finally succeeded in wrapping the sail. I lashed it securely. Then we set the staysail on the short stay, and Molly once again set the course for St. George.

Although he was soaked and exhausted, Ty stubbornly insisted on standing his watch. Ty is almost unflappable on a boat, and he would rather wrestle a shark than wake me when I'm off watch. When he poked his head into the cabin and said softly, but firmly, "John, I hate to do this, but could you come out here for a second?" I knew it must be serious. I quickly slipped on my foul-weather gear and went on deck.

A mysterious, flashing white light would shine every few minutes, sometimes very nearby, and oddly, it appeared to be circling us. It was spooky. I studied the chart, but there was no light marked anywhere near our dead-reckoning position. Finally, the rising moon in the east cast some light on the horizon, and we were able to make out the silhouette of an otherwise unlit submarine. Why was it steering such a wayward course? We did not stick around to find out. We tacked offshore.

At dawn the submarine had disappeared beneath the surface, or beyond the horizon, or had we imagined it? I am convinced that no sensible person can believe the nonsense of the Bermuda Triangle, but you can wonder. We tied up to the quay in quaint St. George, seven days to the hour out of New York City.

Our immediate concern was repairing the furling system. Ty and I spent the morning of October 23 sprawled on our bellies working on it. He unraveled the tangled line and rethreaded it on the drum. He watched carefully as I rolled the headsail in and out several times. It appeared to function properly. Anxious for a quick solution, we reasoned that we must have been carrying too much sail. By placing too great a load on the forestay, we had caused it to vibrate and eventually chafe the line. The obvious, simple solution was to shorten sail sooner in the next gale. We should have known that obvious, simple solutions rarely are the correct ones.

The forestay tension, as well as the complete tune of the rig, had been knocked out of whack. I assumed responsibility for readjusting the rigging. One of the clever design features of the Harken and North system is that to adjust forestay tension, you simply rotate the drum. I removed the lock screws and gave the drum a turn. "Ah, that feels better," I said to myself. Then I gave it another turn. "Ah, that's even better," I thought. "Let's give it one more for good luck." I am known to have the delicate touch of a Russian midwife, and halfway through the third turn, "Thwangggg!" The wires unraveled completely. I'd destroyed the forestay.

Unfortunately, Ty had returned to Detroit the day before. I called several riggers on the island, but because we needed a special swage fitting for the furling gear, they were unable to help us. I called Ty and embarrassedly explained what I had done. He was not overly surprised; after all, he had witnessed my legendary mechanical prowess on many occasions. He said he would find a new forestay and fitting and get it on the next plane to Bermuda.

One of the premier headaches of voyaging has nothing to do with the sea. It is the landlubbing petty bureaucrats who insolently strike fear into anyone who, God forbid, might desire their services. Molly and I spent our entire stay in Bermuda vainly trying to track down an errant funds transfer from my brother Tom. We desperately needed the money to pay a local dentist who had filled one of Molly's aching teeth. No one at the bank, customs, or immigration could figure out what had happened to the money. I finally used my credit card and a phony bank account to raise money at the credit card office in Hamilton. I figured by the time they caught on to the scam, we'd be halfway to Rio. Besides, we were still short a couple of hundred dollars.

Molly and I were shocked to see Ty step off the plane and personally deliver the new forestay. "I figured you might need a hand," he said, smiling. "Besides, I want to make sure you get to Rio." Ty hoisted me up the mast, and I gingerly removed the forestay and wrapped a line around it. Molly walked the bottom of the stay along the quay while I carefully lowered it. Then she and Ty reassembled the furling gear on the new stay, and I hoisted it back into position. Ty insisted on adjusting the tension, and I happily let him.

Ty pitched the bow line aboard and Molly shoved off amidships. "It should be a piece-of-cake sail from here," Ty called from the dock. "Good luck." We quickly cleared narrow St. George's Channel. It was October 30, 1983, and we were bound for Rio de Janeiro, Brazil, 4,500 miles distant.

It was sloppy going as we beat southeast, bucking a stiff easterly wind. We had intentionally ignored a foreboding forecast which called for near gale-force conditions. We were anxious to get moving, and we reasoned that if *Gigi* could not endure a hard blow off Bermuda, how in the hell would she ever tackle Cape Horn and the Southern Ocean?

We shaped a more easterly course as the wind backed to the north of east. *Gigi* drove into the confused seas as the Navik steering vane held a course 35 degrees off the apparent wind. Sailing vast distances is the best way to learn geography. Our route to Rio required us to sail more than halfway across the Atlantic to gain enough easting to clear Brazil's easternmost point at Cape Sao Roque.

According to the pilot chart published by the Defense Mapping Agency and based on more than 100 years of shipping reports, we expected vigorous close reaching as we slashed across the northeast tradewinds. Once we put Bermuda behind us, the chances of encountering a gale were slim. Dodging the equatorial doldrums and determining what meridian to cross the equator at were a challenge. I decided to follow the well-worn path blazed by the clipper ships of the last century and try to cross the line east of the 30th meridian. From Bermuda to the equator we had to traverse 32° of latitude and 35° of longitude.

In the southern hemisphere I hoped we could slacken the sheets, pick up steady, easterly winds, and ride the swift, south setting, Brazilian Current. It was vital to stay well off the coast until we were south of Recife to avoid light, unpredictable winds and contrary currents. Our ambitious goal was to sight Rio's Sugar Loaf Mountain in 35 days by averaging 125 miles daily.

All day long conditions deteriorated. The barometer was falling slowly but steadily. We clung to a true course of 120°. I was feeling wretched and was more or less useless. Molly kept our dead-reckoning plot on the chart, and that was all the navigation we could manage. Fortunately, *Gigi* seems to know when the crew is down and out and she takes care of herself.

During the night of October 30, the furling system pulled its surprising unveiling act and suddenly we had a 150 percent genoa set in gale-force winds. It was my watch, and I staggered forward. Instead of wrestling with the sail, I effected a temporary splice in the furling line and rolled the sail back in. I was furious. I told Molly when we changed watch that I was going to throw the damned system overboard in Rio and revert to conventional, hank-on sails.

Many seasoned sailors urged us not to use roller-furling on the voyage. "It's too unpredictable and unreliable," was the normal complaint. Yet for several, well-thought-out reasons we decided to go with it, and despite the problems we encountered, I would do the same thing again.

Gigi has but 30 inches of freeboard when she is empty and considerably less fully loaded. Her entry is fine and she ships an enormous amount of water over the deck. Working the foredeck can be hazardous, and it is safer and more efficient to control the headsail from the cockpit. Also, sailing shorthanded as we were, the crew is often exhausted, and it is easy to convince yourself not to bother changing headsails. Contrary to what many believe, on shorthanded offshore passages, a reliable, roller-furling system enhances performance. What you lose in sail shape, you gain in instant versatility of sail area. Last but not least, we chose roller furling because it had performed superbly in the English Channel a year before.

October 31 was a repeat of the previous day. The barometer kept falling and the wind kept rising. At noon I was fortunate to snatch a sun sight and total up our first day's run. Despite a seasick captain and tough windward slugging, *Gigi* had clipped off 148 miles. Later in the afternoon, Molly figured out why we were not feeling well. One of the diesel jugs lashed to the stern deck had sprung a leak and was slowly dripping its sickly contents into the cockpit. I cut the lashings and threw the jug overboard, and Molly voraciously scrubbed the cockpit. Occasional breaking waves did the rinsing for her.

Despite relentless Force 8 headwinds, we both felt better after cleaning the boat, and Molly fixed our first hot meal in 36 hours. Just as she handed me a cup of steaming beef stew, the damn furling line chafed through and released the genoa again. *Gigi* lurched to starboard and I dashed forward. I could not splice the line because it was wrapped inside the drum. We had to drop the sail, and in a hurry, before it flogged itself to death.

Molly steered into the wind and let the halyard fly. I pulled wildly and succeeded in lowering the sail nearly to the deck before the luff jammed in the slot. I lashed the head of the sail to the stay and the rest of it to the lifeline. Then I set the headsail on the short stay once again. I resolved to deal with the furling system when conditions improved, and went back to the cockpit for another cup of stew.

The barometer kept falling during the night, and the old sailor's axiom, "Long foretold, long last," proved true. The winds increased to 45 knots. The gray, ugly dawn that crept above the horizon on November 1, 1983, made me question my motives, as well as my sanity, for leaving Bermuda. Powerful, breaking seas clobbered *Gigi* and frequently swept over the length of her. We were determined not to lose our hard-fought easting, and I remembered my lessons learned in the Caribbean and English Channel. We weren't going to heave-to or run off unless it was absolutely necessary. We were just not going to give in to the gale. The sea merely laughed at us.

Approximately 250 miles southeast of Bermuda, the storm reached its height, Force 10 (48- to 55-knot winds, 20- to 30-foot seas). Molly and I were exhausted. For two and a half days we had kept *Gigi* on course, but it had come at the expense of sleep. We could not afford another sleepless night, but to sleep, somehow we had to ease the violent, crashing motion aboard.

I carefully clipped on my safety harness and inched forward by sliding along the coachroof on my fanny. First, I tied the third reef into the mainsail, and then I lowered the staysail. Molly set the Navik to steer 60° to 70° off the wind. Our speed slowed to 2 knots, but the motion was drastically improved. We were confident that we could ride out the remainder of the tempest without losing much ground to leeward.

I was slow assuming my watch duty at 8:00 P.M. (2000 hours) and the two hours in the cockpit seemed endless. The powerful wind whipped the tops of the waves into driving spray that virtually eliminated all visibility. When I shined a flashlight on my watch, I was relieved to see that it was nearly 10:00 P.M. I only had the end of watch ritual, pumping the bilge, before I could collapse into the dry bunk Molly was warming for me. I cautiously crept to the back of the cockpit and started to pump. "Damn," I thought to myself, "it's full. It will need at least 100 strokes to empty it." The sea never gave me the chance.

I heard the wave before I saw it. It crested with a thunderous roar. I spun around to starboard and caught an unforgettable glimpse of a 20-foot wall of water, steeply curled and poised to break. Instinctively, I dove for the companionway, even though two of three hatchboards were secured. The wave unleashed its fury and crashed into *Gigi* amidships, knocking her over like a toy in a bathtub. I clutched the mainsheet as she went over.

The few seconds that I was completely submerged seemed like an eternity. Miraculously, the tether on my safety harness held, and as the lead in *Gigi*'s keel forced her upright, I came up with her. I climbed back aboard over the crushed leeward stanchions and lifelines.

I immediately called out for Molly and pulled wildly at the hatch-boards. She was buried beneath a pile of books, clothes, pots, pans, and sails. One moment she'd been lying in her berth, and the next she was pinned to the ceiling as *Gigi* rolled over at least 150 degrees. Amazingly, she was not injured.

When I realized we both were OK, my reaction was strange. I was furious. There hadn't been time to be afraid. I shouted obscenities at the sea. I noticed the triple-reefed mainsail with the boastful "Cape Horn 270°" lying limp along the boom. How could the ocean ruin my grand plans with one rogue wave?

The cabin was flooded with water more than a foot above the sole. Molly thought we must have been holed or that we stove in a port, and that I was yelling for her to gather up the emergency kit and prepare to abandon ship. She stumbled up the companionway steps, struggling to lift our 75-pound emergency kit into the cockpit.

"No, no, baby. We're not going down. The ocean isn't taking us yet," I assured her, although I had no assurance that what I was saying was true. "We better start pumping though." Both buckets and the bilge handle had been washed away. Molly grabbed the large pressure cooker and started to empty the water in the cabin into the cockpit, which had finally drained. I found a large screwdriver to use as a bilge handle and started to pump. Another wave clobbered *Gigi* and I realized we couldn't just let her drift aimlessly. I brought her before the wind and went to the stern to engage the steering vane. I was shocked to see the water pendulum, a fiberglass paddle on a stainless-steel shaft, broken in half. The vane was rendered useless.

I concentrated all of my energy on steering *Gigi* before the enormous rollers that piled up astern. Molly pitched pot after pot of water out of the cabin. *Gigi* surged down the faces of the waves at 10 knots, and I battled the tiller in the troughs to keep her from dangerously

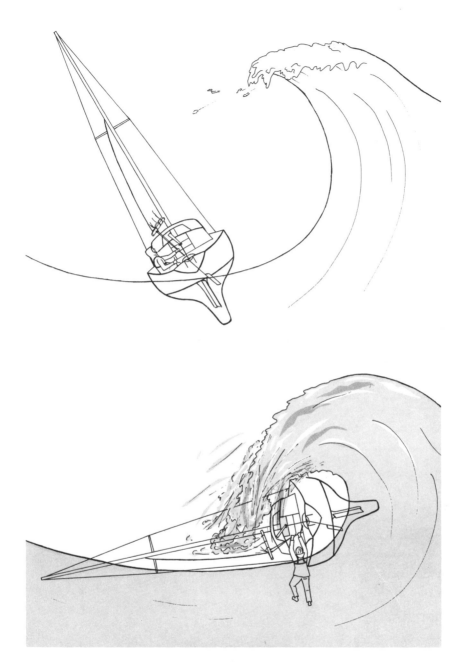

Two hundred and fifty miles southeast of Bermuda, Gigi was overwhelmed by a rogue wave. Harnessed alone in the cockpit, John hears a thunderous roar and glancing to starboard, sees a 20- to 30-foot wall of water. The wave breaks and crashes over Gigi, pitching John overboard. Frantically, John clutches the mainsheet. He is completely submerged (next page) as Gigi rolls over 160 degrees. When Gigi rights herself, John is saved by his safety harness. Back on her feet, Gigi is still afloat, and, miraculously, her mast is still standing. As John climbs back aboard, he notices that the mainsail is ripped, the steering vane is crushed, and the dodger is flattened like a pancake.

rounding up. I quickly learned that it was best to keep the seas about 10 degrees off the stern, to starboard. In between waves, I pumped the bilge frantically, but one nasty wave rose up over the stern while I was pumping, and before I could steer off, it overran us. The surging water pooped us and flooded the cockpit and cabin again.

"Enough, damn it, enough. Leave us alone," I cried at the dark, violent ocean around us. Tears streamed down my face and my body shivered. Suddenly, there was plenty of time to be afraid.

6

Headwinds and Headaches

*W*E ALTERNATED STEERING AND pumping in hourly stints. Around midnight, after we'd emptied most of the water out of the boat, I staggered below. The cabin was a shambles with gear spewn about everywhere. The destructive force of a single wave had turned our orderly little world into a chaotic nightmare.

The cushions on the berths were soaked, our sleeping bags were soaked, everything was soaked. I spread the storm trysail out on the cabin sole and lay down. I propped my head on a soggy cushion and pulled my foul-weather jacket over my head. Eventually, I drifted into a fitful sleep.

I dreamt to the eerie rhythm of a John Masefield poem. The sea ballad, "Cape Horn Gospel — I," tells the tale of an ordinary seaman, Bill. Early in the voyage, poor old Bill dies, and the crew wraps his bones in a tarpaulin and pitches him over the side. Later, as the ship nears the Horn, old Bill's ghost comes back aboard.

> *"I'm weary of them there mermaids*
> *old Bill's ghost says to me.*
> *It ain't no place for a Christian*
> *below there — under the sea.*
> *For it's all blown sand and shipwrecks*
> *and old bones eaten bare*
> *and them cold, fishy females*
> *with long, green weeds for hair."*

In a flash I was flailing in the water again. Frantically, I reached for an outstretched hand, the welcome hand of a mermaid. Just before I grasped her lifesaving hand, she changed into an ugly, green sea monster, with, yep, you guessed it, long green weeds for hair and seawater oozing from her mouth. I woke up screaming. When I checked my watch, it was time to relieve Molly.

In the morning, with the light of another day, we took stock of our situation. Structurally, *Gigi* seemed intact. Her fiberglass hull was still in one piece and her mast still stood tall. However, a quick survey of her equipment was very disheartening. The steering vane was out of commission, and the heavy-weather mainsail had three gaping tears at the reef points. The spray dodger had been flattened like a pancake, and the running lights, antennas, and wind instruments on the masthead were lost. A lot of smaller items — winch and bilge handles, buckets, etc. — had obviously been washed out of the cockpit.

Bleary eyed, we ran before the moderating storm, toward the west, for 24 hours. Fortunately, the autopilot, our backup to the steering vane, still worked and steered a steady course before the wind. But when Molly tried to conjure up a hot meal, she disgustedly added the clogged kerosene stove to the growing list of casualties.

At dawn on November 5, the winds had decreased to 20 knots and the seas were more manageable. I went forward and bent on the spare mainsail. Then I set the staysail to steady the boat as I tried, in vain, to raise the genoa. Luckily, I'd saved the genoa by securely lashing it to the netting along the forward lifelines before the capsize. However, the aluminum forestay extrusions were bent by the force of the water about 15 feet up from the tack. Molly steered into the wind and I hauled on the halyard, but each time the luff of the sail jammed at or before the bend as the sail flapped wildly in the wind. Finally, my waterlogged brain reminded me that we had an alternative.

Ty had wisely insisted that all of our headsails be fitted with grommets every couple of feet along the luff. Together with an ingenious yet simple canvas strap developed by North Sails, called a luff stop, it was possible to lash the sails to the forestay, over the extrusions, and hoist them in a conventional manner. I decided to raise the 105 percent jib instead of the genoa and leave the staysail set. By sailing *Gigi* as a cutter, we had the option of dousing the jib and carrying on with just the staysail if the winds piped up in a hurry.

We set the course for Rio de Janeiro for the first time in days, but truthfully, the thought of continuing on to Rio was staggering. I had a difficult decision to make: Should we call in for repairs? Molly and I went below to discuss our alternatives. I mixed a couple of stiff gin tangoes (gin and Tang, warm) and opened a can of tuna.

"John," Molly began, "I don't think we should press on, not in the condition we're in . . . . Oh shit, damn!" *Gigi* lurched to port and Molly spilled her drink. "Oh, baby, I'm so tired," Molly sobbed. "You told me this was supposed to be the suntan leg." I put my arm around her and she rested her head on my chest.

"You're right, Molly. Hell, Rio is still more or less 4,500 miles away, although I don't really know where we are. And the damage . . . it would be stupid to carry on. But, well, I don't know . . . I hate to give up." The epitome of a decisive captain.

The truth was, and I knew it, that *Gigi* had survived the capsize remarkably well and was surely capable of continuing on. But there was more than just broken equipment to consider. Our spirits were broken too, and a broken spirit is far more crippling than a broken steering vane. I scanned the small-scale chart on the navigation desk and decided that St. Thomas, in the Virgin Islands, was the logical port of refuge. It was approximately 600 miles south of our "very estimated" position and a good port for repairs.

"What do you say we head for good, old St. Thomas, Mol?"

She smiled at me and said, "I'll mix us another drink."

Amazingly, the Stephens single-sideband radio still hummed when I flicked the switch, and we were able to transmit because we relied on the insulated backstay for the antenna. The radio I had once ridiculed as an extravagant gadget allowed us to relay the news of our stormy ordeal and our change in plans to all those concerned on the mainland. I reached Ty, and he agreed to meet us in St. Thomas to help repair *Gigi* and bring a load of replacement parts.

As we shaped a southerly course toward the Caribbean, retracing the route we sailed in *Epoch* three years before, I became ornery and hard to live with. I couldn't help but second-guess my decision; I viewed it as a retreat, and I felt that I was throwing in the towel on the entire expedition. The dreary, blustery weather accentuated my despair. How would we ever attain our goal of reaching San Francisco in 120 sailing days? The Golden Gate Bridge seemed farther away than the moon.

I craved a cup of hot coffee, but I could not prompt the finicky stove to spark a flame. Slowly, a little at a time, we cleaned up the colossal mess in the cabin. Molly described the stinky interior as having "the sweet, combined fragrance of sour fruit; wet, dirty laundry; and diesel fumes." We tacked a "must fix" list to the bulkhead, and it grew to four pages before we made port.

Gigi finally found the northeast tradewinds on November 6, and the sky cleared at twilight. Anxious for an accurate position fix as we neared land, I shot three sights on seven different stars and plotted all 21 LOPs. The plotting sheet looked more like a lofting diagram, but I had a pretty good idea where we were. We raced the rising sun into St. Thomas Harbor on November 8, 1983.

Ty was on the dock at the Yacht Haven Marina, and he snatched our docklines as I eased *Gigi* into a slip. After a 24-hour hiatus, half of which we spent getting drunk and the other half sobering up, we started putting *Gigi* back together. We worked furiously in uncharacteristically hot, humid weather. Luckily, a former employee of The Navigation School, Scott Palmer, was the manager of a local charter company, and he helped coordinate our repairs.

The local North Sail loft picked up and patched our tattered mainsail and also repaired the forestay extrusions. We installed a new steering vane and replaced the stove burners. A marine electrician sent me up to the masthead (he was afraid of heights), and, following his careful instructions, I mounted new running lights and a new antenna. We replaced most of the items we'd lost and gave *Gigi* a thorough cleaning. One week to the day after we arrived, *Gigi* was shipshape and ready to put to sea.

On November 15, we beat across the Anegada Passage in light conditions and then threaded a course between St. Martin and St. Barts. East of St. Barts, we tacked south as the wind remained light from the southeast. Molly and I were dragging. The week in St. Thomas had been hectic, and we were experiencing a delayed reaction as we stumbled about the deck in slow motion.

We held our southerly heading through the night of November 17, and in the morning we were abeam the leeward shore of Antigua. I went below to put the teakettle on the stove, but I was nearly overpowered by diesel fumes. We had been charging the batteries all morning, and I quickly hollered at Molly to shut down the engine. Fuel was leaking all over the place. I removed the floorboards and was horrified to find the bilge full of diesel fuel! Somehow, someway, we'd sprung a leak in the fuel system. I checked the gauge on the panel, and sure enough, the fuel supply needle hovered below the E. We had lost our entire 20 gallons of fuel. I wanted to cry.

Reluctantly, we altered course for English Harbor. "This is just what we need. I can't believe it," I complained to Molly, as I inflated the dinghy. "Before we even look at that stupid engine we need a beer." We rowed ashore at once.

"Shouldn't we make sure the anchor is holding?" Molly asked.

"Let the boat drift away, I don't care."

Sipping a cold Heineken on the veranda of the old Officers' Quarters at Nelson's Dockyard, I asked Molly if she thought we should postpone the expedition for a year. "I mean, everything that can go wrong has gone wrong," I griped. Molly shrugged, then she said, "John, it's up to you, but I don't think you could live with yourself for a year if you quit now."

In the afternoon, we attacked the little Yanmar diesel with a vengeance. Molly cleaned the bilge and I found the guilty part, a leaky fuel pump (lift pump). Wedged into a quarter berth that was designed for midgets, I cursed Jeremy Rogers (the boat's builder) as I tried to remove the pump. My thick, undexterous fingers kept dropping the wrench, and finally Molly took my place. She popped the pump off the engine in a minute, and wondered what I had been swearing about.

"Never mind, let's just fix it."

We replaced a worn gasket, and then optimistically installed the pump again. I fired up the engine while Molly watched for leakage. "Stop, stop, stop!" she yelled. It still leaked. The seal around the pump was shot. We needed a new pump. There was no chance of finding the pump we needed in Antigua. There was only one thing to do; call Ty. I have never dreaded a phone call more, but I had to do it; we had to get moving. I rowed ashore and called.

"Hi, Ty."

"John? Are you on land?"

"Um, well, sort of, I mean, uh, yes, I guess I am."

"What's the problem?"

Oh, boy, here it comes, I thought. "Ty, you are not going to believe this." I prepped him before I explained the dilemma. I expected him to be upset, but he wasn't. In fact, he was cheerful and tried to cheer me up. He said he would send a pump on the next flight to Antigua. Time and again during the long course of our journey, Ty dipped into his pocketbook to keep *Gigi* going. And time and again, he dipped into his reserve of spirit to keep his young, wavering captain going. Ty had some shocking news of his own.

Chay Blyth's trimaran, *Beefeater,* had been abandoned by his transatlantic delivery crew. *Beefeater* was lost and he had had to scuttle his voyage. Fortunately, the three crewmen were rescued.

The new pump arrived on November 23, and we promptly installed it. In the morning we took on fuel and water, and set off for Rio de Janeiro for the third time. By detouring to the Caribbean islands, we had added about 600 miles to the voyage, and had also made the 3,800-mile passage to Rio much more difficult.

From Antigua, our desired true course for the first 2,000 miles was 120°, a southeast heading. That meant we were forced to battle the relentless northeast tradewinds head-on. I anticipated a prolonged windward slug, but I never imagined it would turn into such a marathon of endurance.

The first three days out were peaceful and lulled us into believing that I was overestimating the difficulty of the passage. *Gigi* clung to a tight southeast heading as the gentle, Force 3 wind blew from the east. We managed just over 100 miles each day. It is so easy to take the lovely sailing days for granted; somehow the storms clutter up your memory. But the night of November 25 reminded me why I am compelled to leave my natural, secure habitat on land and take to the sea in small boats.

Gigi eased along, right on course, dancing across shining wavelets. After the sun made a glorious curtain call off to the west, the bright stars of twilight took the stage. Darkness descended and the stars aligned themselves in familiar patterns above. Shooting stars blazed lingering trails throughout the heavens, and I felt a strong kinship with mariners of all epochs. Just before the conclusion of my first watch at 2300 hours, the moon nosed above the eastern horizon. Moonrises are mysterious; is it a ship? Is it a voyager from another galaxy?

When I resumed my watch at 0200, the moon was high in the sky. I made up a little jingle to sing:

> *"The steady glow of earth's distant satellite*
> *casts a silhouette upon the dark horizon.*
> Sirius, *the dog star, burns a bluish bright*
> *As Orion the Hunter, guides* Gigi *through the night."*

(Fortunately, as a reader, you are spared my vocal rendition!) I wouldn't have traded places with anybody on the planet that night. Just a couple of days later, however, I would have greedily traded places with just about anybody on this planet or any other.

The tradewinds gradually strengthened and the ride became rougher. *Gigi* heeled hard to starboard, 20 to 30 degrees, constantly, as she beat to windward, 30 degrees off the apparent wind. On the fourth day of the passage we prematurely started dreaming about easing the sheets, but thickening weather, accompanying a low-pressure system, had other ideas. The tradewinds finally rolled up their sleeves and blew as tradewinds should blow — 20 to 25 knots. It was hard to find a dry seat in the cockpit as *Gigi* plunged her nose into the building seas and kicked up spray. Still, we were making steady progress, and during our first week at sea I was satisfied to average 108 miles daily.

Life aboard took a turn for the worse on December 2, the eighth day out of Antigua. The tropical sun gave way to dismal gray clouds, and we were forced to tack to the northeast as the wind insisted on blowing from the southeast. The seas heaped up and tossed *Gigi* about like dirty laundry in a washing machine. After her first watch, Molly wrote in the log:

> *"I don't know how the boat stays together; we come off some of these waves like lemmings off a cliff."*

Then she obviously glanced over at me and added:

> *"I can't believe he can sleep through this!"*

Day in and day out, *Gigi* bashed to windward. We chose the most opportune heading out of the eastern quadrant, depending on the wind direction. We fought tenaciously to maintain adequate sea room off the South American coast, and we laid a track 350 miles northeast of the mouth of the Amazon River. The confused seas were the primary cause of our discomfort; windward sailing in steep seas is exhausting.

At noon on December 3, I was shocked to plot our position 139 miles farther along on the chart. It didn't seem possible; the knotmeter never registered more than 5 knots, and frequently a lot less as *Gigi* plunged into powerful waves. On December 4 we reeled off 165 miles, noon to noon, and I realized something mysterious was happening; *Gigi* was making 7 knots upwind and up current!

My initial thought was that something was wrong with my sextant. "Ah ha, something is definitely wrong here," I mumbled as I raised the instrument to the sun. "Half of the sun is missing." I checked and rechecked the alignment of the mirrors and adjusted the index error, but everything lined up properly. I scratched my head, and went below to work out the sights and plot our position again to see if I could find the error. When I opened up the Nautical Almanac, I realized that my sextant was just fine; the sun was being partially eclipsed by the moon!

But our phenomenal progress was not the result of an annular eclipse; instead, a close inspection of the pilot chart revealed that we had luckily stumbled into a favorable current. A thin, east setting, equatorial countercurrent flowed between the broad, northeast tradewind or Canary Current to the north and the equatorial current to the south. The countercurrent boosted our daily runs by as much as 60 miles.

Despite the tremendous boost to our progress, we cursed the current as much as we praised it. The collision of the east-flowing current and the contrary tradewinds caused the nasty seas that made life aboard hellish. A series of mechanical mishaps heightened our frustration.

On December 5, the diesel overheated as we charged the batteries. I shut it down as the overheat alarm sang out. Molly suggested I check the strainer on the seawater intake valve. I closed the seacock and removed the strainer. Sure enough, it was clogged with seaweeds and barnacles. Molly scraped it clean with a wire brush and I replaced it. Molly then hit the start button and the engine rumbled into life. I sniffed around the engine compartment for a while and thought to myself, "So far, so good. That must have been the problem." A minute later, I announced to Molly, "That did it, let's get some air."

Just as we climbed into the cockpit, the overheat alarm triggered. I dashed below and Molly killed the engine. Something was burning; the burning rubber was unmistakable. I pulled open the companionway, but the fire was already over. The exhaust hose was smoldering in the rear of the compartment, but there wasn't a flame. Fortunately, venting the compartment was enough to cool down the engine, but I was steaming, wondering what the problem might be. Then it hit me. "The seacock, I forgot to open the seacock!" The worst part of the accident was that the engine was temporarily waylaid, at least until conditions moderated and we could patch the exhaust hose.

The following day, the kerosene stove burners clogged up again. I spent all day tinkering with the burners; we had much too far to go to be without hot food. Molly remarked that I took the stove crisis more seriously than the engine, and she was right. The thought of crunchy, cold noodles for 30 days was all the inspiration I needed. Finally, just before dinner, I had both burners purring and throwing beautiful blue flames.

Throughout the passage, the roller-furling gear continued its surprising unveiling acts. Though the situation was never critical, it was always aggravating. We rigged up various fairleads and chafe guards at the drum, but nothing seemed to prevent the furling line from eventually wearing thin. In desperation, after we'd used all the ¼-inch line aboard, we rethreaded the drum with ⅜-inch line. The thicker line made all the difference, as it wrapped smoothly around the drum and was more chafe resistant.

Molly hit the wall on the night of December 6. She slammed the bulkhead as she struggled into her berth and cried out, "I don't want to be here tonight!" I chastised her for being a baby, but she told me to shut up. To spite me, she said tersely, "Tonight I am going to dream about a

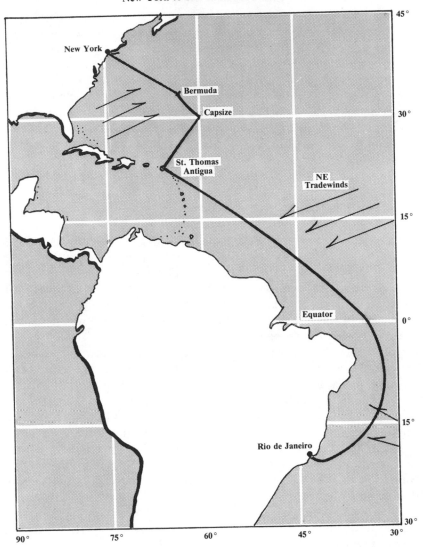

house in the country and a dog.'' Then she pulled the sleeping bag over her head.

The noon sight the next day helped revive Molly's morale. We had pounded our way 152 miles, and Molly seized the day and snapped out of the blues. With a flurry of activity, she baked a couple of loaves of fresh bread, which was a challenge in the rough conditions with our cranky stove. That night she brewed up a heaping batch of spaghetti and meatballs, and even a chocolate cake for dessert. Our rising spirits peaked the next day when I calculated our noon to noon run at 167 miles, upwind!

On December 9, I felt we had enough easting to start heading south toward the equator.

Just when the benevolent countercurrent had thrust us back into the thick of the clipper ship race, and just when Molly and I had begun to fantasize about a Christmas Day arrival in Rio, we encountered the equatorial doldrums. The winds lost their steam as we sailed south, but they insisted on blowing over the bow. Sailors are such a fickle lot; as soon as our progress slowed, I told Molly, "I'd prefer getting my brains knocked out and sailing 167 miles." Molly disagreed. My mood was directly proportional to our progress, and Molly's mood was directly proportional to the angle of heel.

Geographically, the doldrums straddle the equator, north and south. The maximum width of the low-pressure belt is about 1,000 miles, and if you're lucky, the minimum width is about 300 miles. Choosing the proper meridian to pierce the doldrums is like tossing a dart at a world map; it's largely a matter of luck.

Meteorologically, the doldrums are a dreadful region to traverse under sail. It was as though we had drifted into a cave of low, dense cloud cover. Violent, 50-knot gusts interrupted eerie, frustrating calms. December 11 was a typical doldrum day. In the morning I spilled my cereal all over the chart. After lunch I repaired the exhaust hose, but as I administered a quart of oil, I spilled it all over the engine. Then I spilled the bilge cleaner I was using to clean up the oil, all over the cabin sole!

Gigi slipped through the doldrums without much delay. We crossed the equator just east of the 35th meridian on December 12. The noon sight confirmed our position south of the line. On December 14, a patch of brilliant blue penetrated the thick clouds, and we followed it like a flickering candle at the mouth of the cave and sailed into the crystal clear skies of the southern hemisphere.

I had hoped to clear the eastern end of Fernando de Noronha, a small, offshore island 300 miles southeast of the equator. The winds had other intentions, and we were forced to beat to the southwest. In the end, we cleared Cape Sao Roque, the easternmost point of the South American mainland, by just 8 to 9 miles.

Once we were abeam Recife, we had clear sailing all the way to Rio. On December 17, for the first time in 23 days, we eased the sheets and *Gigi* romped south on a reach. The wind clocked around to the north, and on December 18 we set the spinnaker for the first time since the second day out of New York. We had to adjust to the yawing, rolling motion of downwind sailing, but it was an adjustment we were happy to make. The ultimate luxury, however, was to open the center hatch and ventilate the cabin.

I also had to adjust to the southern hemisphere stars. Arcux and Gacrux, the pillars of the Southern Cross, burned brightly to the south, all night long. Canopus, the second brightest star in the sky and the foundation for the constellation Carina, the ship's keel, was our steering star. Both the days and the nights were clear, and we dug out the movie camera and captured ourselves raising the spinnaker, baking bread, and goofing around. Sailing was fun again.

On December 22 we capped a great week of sailing with a 151-mile run. Our weekly total was just under 1,000 miles as we averaged 136 miles daily. We were less than 400 miles from Rio de Janeiro.

But the Atlantic Ocean still had one more trick up its sleeve. On the night of December 23, the weather turned squally just as we sailed into a Texas-style, offshore oilfield. Most of the rigs were lit up like Christmas trees, but the chart warned us about possible unlit derelicts and pipes. During the brief squalls, it would pour and virtually eliminate all visibility, and we were compelled to heave-to or risk running into a rig. On December 24 we left the last rig astern and closed on the coast; it looked as though a Christmas Day arrival was imminent.

Just after dawn, the prominent peak of Cape Buzios decorated the distant horizon. Land ho! Off the starboard bow. After 30 days at sea, the lush, green mountains lured us like magnets. Late on Christmas Eve we skirted Cape Frio and tacked to the west for the approach to Rio, 60 miles down the coast. The wind held all night, and we charged for the finishing line of the first leg.

On Christmas morning the wind simply vanished. *Gigi* was becalmed just 30 miles away from a cold beer and a freshwater shower. The fuel gauge was well below empty, and I did not want to run the engine dry and clog up the injectors with sludge off the bottom of the tank. "Well, it looks like we'll have to sit and wait for the wind to come up," I told Molly. Then I got a brainstorm. "Hey, wait a minute, baby," I said excitedly, as I flung open the cockpit locker and pulled out the jug of kerosene. I shook it. "All right! There are at least a couple of gallons in here."

"What are you doing, you idiot? That's kerosene." Molly thought I had lost my marbles. "You've been at sea too long."

"You're right, and I don't want to spend another day out here either," I said, as I poured the kerosene into the tank. "Molly, our little Yanmar is going to love this highly refined diesel fuel known as kerosene. Now start that engine."

Just after noon, we powered into beautiful Guanabara Bay, 31 days out of Antigua. *Gigi* was back in the thick of the Cape Horn clipper ship race, and the first leg was finally behind us.

7

The War Zone

GUANABARA BAY IS A beautiful natural harbor. Verdant mountains, sandy beaches, and Rio de Janeiro's towering skyline circle the bay. The sheltered bay gradually widens from 1 mile at the mouth to 15 miles at the head, and is one of South America's busiest ports. As *Gigi* sliced through the light mist, Molly and I felt the incomparable satisfaction of a passage well done. We moored *Gigi* Mediterranean-style at the Marina del Gloria near the center of the city. A Christmas Day arrival gave us a legitimate excuse to forego the usual aggravation of clearing customs. Instead, we flagged down a taxi and headed out to Copacabana Beach, where we hoped to find Ty.

The taxi driver dropped us off at the opulent Copacabana Palace Hotel. Molly suggested we inquire about Ty at the front desk, but I had a better idea. We went straight to the bar, and sure enough, we spotted him at a table in the back. He was delighted but surprised to see us; he did not expect us for at least another week. We'd been mysteriously out of radio contact during the latter part of the passage, and he could only guess at our ETA. Ty immediately ordered a round of drinks. Although Molly and I were thirsting for a cold beer, he insisted we try the local favorite, a sweet whiskey and lime mix called a caipirinha.

My chair swayed beneath me, and I had a tendency to clutch my drink as it rested on the table. I expected the room to heel hard to starboard at any moment. Ty was eager to hear about our passage. He was in great spirits, a combination of caipirinhas and anticipation had him bubbling with enthusiasm. He interrupted our yarning long enough to tell us that we might have company off Cape Horn. Mike Kane, a highly accomplished multihull sailor from California, and two crewmembers had left New York shortly after *Gigi* in Kane's 56-foot trimaran, *Crusader*. Kane, like Chay Blyth before him, was bound for San Francisco in pursuit of *Flying Cloud*'s long-standing record of 89 days and 21 hours. The last report Ty had had from the editors of *Yacht Racing & Cruising* was that *Crusader* was days ahead of the record pace and charging for the Horn.

Ty had been in Rio for a couple of weeks. He had decided to combine business with pleasure (if our voyage could be called pleasurable!) and investigate Rio's investment opportunities while he waited for us. Ty is a successful importer of auto-related parts, and Brazil's favorable exchange rate and pro-export policies enticed him. However, Rio de Janeiro has a way of sidetracking even the most ardent capitalist with its frustrating "tomorrow" attitude. Ty concluded that the investment opportunities were marginal at best, but the beaches, nightclubs, and other attractions were unmatched!

The first day ashore after a long passage has a dreamlike quality. The hours drag on, and although your body is bone weary, sleep seems impossible. We drank late into the evening and satisfied all of our culinary cravings at an all-you-can-eat "churrascaria" restaurant. From the moment you sit down until the time you leave, waiters dash between tables with long skewers of beef, pork, and veal. They slice generous portions onto your plate and then sprint off to the next table. Ty won a $5 wager when even I had to finally say, "Nao mais."

Ty had lugged two heavy duffle bags with him on the plane, but unfortunately, the bags were impounded at the airport. The customs officers wanted tangible proof that a yacht named *Gigi* truly existed before they would release the bags. The country's economy is reeling under the burden of massive, overdue foreign debts and a spiraling inflation rate. The government is paranoid about foreign goods entering the country and has established an import moratorium on nearly everything. Until Ty could present *Gigi*'s clearance papers, the bags remained locked in a shed at the airport.

Even with the proper papers it was still a struggle to secure the bags. Ty tackled the job, knowing that my lack of patience with bureaucrats generally compounds the problem. He wasted two days filing forms and watching them get shuffled from desk to desk before he finally returned to the boat with the bags in tow. He was furious. "If the damned idiots had just looked inside the bags," he said in exasperation, "they would have seen that this stuff is designed for the Arctic! Why would I smuggle Arctic survival suits into Brazil?" I wiped the sweat from my brow and sympathized with him.

Once we sorted out the gear in the bags, it was easy to understand Ty's concern; they were stuffed with thousands of dollars worth of clothing and equipment. For starters, he had two custom-fitted survival suits, a set of heavy-duty Henry Lloyd foul-weather gear, and a complete line of Patagonia polypropylene-pile undergarments for each of us. He also had a new forestay and roller-furling drum. He had jib sheets, tide tables, charts, and specially packaged foods. Ty did not skimp on anything; *Gigi* and her crew were well prepared for their encounter with the mighty Southern Ocean.

Nobly, the three of us resisted most of Rio's pre-carnival temptations. We spent two weeks working furiously in 100-degree temperatures. Cape Horn has a disturbing knack of making even the most frivolous chores serious. The exciting crew of the *Gigi* would usually collapse into bed before 9:00 P.M., the time when most of Rio's trendy residents were just coming to life.

Gradually, we chipped away at our "repair and replace" list, and *Gigi* began to look like a yacht that had at least a reasonable chance of besting Cape Horn. Unfortunately, the three of us were, for the most part, mechanical hacks, and many projects took longer than they should have. Ty and I replaced the forestay after mounting a new, chafe-resistant, Harken furling drum. We struggled to secure a Norseman fitting to the head of the stay. We cursed and complained as we tried to bend the wires around the steel terminal. Luckily, Bennit, the owner of an impeccable yawl which we rafted alongside, was watching us.

"Please excuse me," he said, "but do you mind?" He leaped ashore with his tool bag and promptly redid the job Ty and I had butchered.

"This is very important, no?" he asked.

"Yes, it holds up the mast," Ty responded.

"I know," Bennit said, nodding his head. "But it is OK now. It will hold, but, my friends, please do not test it at Cape Horn."

Bennit harbored grave doubts about our ambitious intentions, and more than once, tried to talk us out of it. He even had an Argentine friend of his, Renee, the captain of a freighter, strike fear into our hearts with his stories of the Southern Ocean. To their dismay, they could not dissuade us, and I think, secretly, they both longed to ship aboard *Gigi* and join us.

Together with his wife and son, Bennit was rebuilding *Anegulus,* a graceful 50-footer designed by German Frers. They were preparing for a voyage north to America. Bennit had been an executive with IBM of Brazil — a member of the board of directors and just a few rungs below the presidency — when he decided to chuck it all and take to the high seas. The wavering policies of the military government and high-level corruption were the reasons he was leaving his homeland. "Until this continent can weed out the corrupt, we will never catch up to the rest of the world," he told us with great sadness.

Another local resident became intrigued with our voyage and helped us tremendously. Alexander Levi, a multihull enthusiast who was a member of Brazil's 1972 Olympic sailing team, helped us track down spare parts and acted as our interpreter. He invited us to his house for dinner on December 29, and we had a delightful evening. His home was high up in the hills overlooking the bay, and his family was charming. After dinner Alexander played a video tape of the 1982 Whitbread Around the World Race. Shivers went up my spine as I watched 60- and 70-foot maxis shuddering under the force of Southern Ocean waves. What would Cape Horn conjure up in the way of adversity for tiny *Gigi*?

New Year's Eve was an exception to our early-to-bed, early-to-rise policy. We took the day off. Molly and I were already anticipating the pain of separation, which loomed just ahead. After the sun set, Ty and a few friends went off to a samba while Molly and I joined the masses along Copacabana Beach. Usually we abhor crowds, but this night was special. It was strangely comforting to be among more than a million people on a beach, fellow human beings, all celebrating the arrival of yet another new year.

Nineteen hundred and eighty-four was dawning. I was bound for Cape Horn and beyond. Molly was destined for the drudgery of land life back in the States. I wanted to say so much, but I didn't. I held her hand and thought about the other times we had been separated for long periods; somehow we've always managed to draw even closer as a result. After a spectacular fireworks display signalled the midnight hour, we walked back to our room and held each other all night long.

The day before Molly's flight back to America, Ty treated us to a crew dinner at Maxim's of Paris (in Rio). Molly looked smashing in a sophisticated silk white jump suit, and even Ty and I managed to look respectable in suits and ties. Dinner was delicate and delicious, and afterward we retired to the balcony for brandy and cigars. With Hennessey running around my head, and a little high from a strong cigar, I had a desperate urge to begin our voyage. If Ty had not ordered another bottle, I would have convinced them both to set sail that night.

On January 4, Molly and I took a taxi to the airport. We were late and there wasn't time to be melancholy before her flight was announced. I carried her suitcase to the security checkpoint, and she whispered in my ear, "Sail hard, my lover, and don't worry — you were made to sail around Cape Horn. I love you."

"I love you too, Mol. Take care, baby. Goodbye."

She was gone. I watched her plane taxi into position and then take to the skies. Working on the boat, the time had slipped by and I had not said the things I should have. I was never more lonely in my life.

On January 6, Ty and I provisioned. We were the essence of innocence in the sprawling, fragrant market. Our Portuguese was pathetic, and the English/Portuguese dictionary was little help. We tried to determine the contents of the cans by the pictures on the labels. When Ty overheard an elderly lady mumbling in English, he latched onto her. She laughed at our odd assortment of canned goods and happily helped us replace many items we'd chosen by mistake. Our six enormous jars of peanut butter turned out to be pickled mustard! When we returned to the boat and stowed everything aboard, *Gigi* sank below her second bootstripe line. The forepeak was stuffed from the cushions to the deck, and we had to set up lee cloths to keep many other items in the salon berths. We took on fuel and water at the yacht club on the morning of January 7, 1984. "OK, Ty, let go the bow line." Sluggishly, *Gigi* made her way for the open ocean.

Clear of Guanabara Bay, we pointed *Gigi*'s bow south toward the bottom of the world. The ocean was placid and the air hung heavy as *Gigi* rumbled along to the rhythm of her two-cylinder diesel. Slowly, the hotel-laden coastline faded from view. We were disgusted by the debris in the water; even 20 miles offshore the ocean was sabotaged by ugly flotsam. Rio de Janeiro is blessed with a beautiful natural environment, but the residents have no concept of ecological conservation. The city is littered, and the air and water are quickly being polluted. It is a pity; why can't we learn from our mistakes?

The going was very light, and as I guided *Gigi* over a calm sea, I chuckled at a letter from my brother, Tom. He advised us to go through the Straits of Magellan instead of rounding Cape Horn. "Who will know?" he asked.

I prefer to start a long passage uneventfully. The easy motion allowed Ty to find his sea legs. I felt at home back aboard *Gigi*; I slept better in my cramped berth than I had in a luxurious hotel bed.

We angled across busy coastal shipping lanes during the night, and in the morning a light wind emerged from the north. I went forward to set the spinnaker, and as I fumbled with the various sheets and guys I noticed a few dolphins playing off the bow. I hauled up the chute and *Gigi* came alive. Suddenly the sea came alive as well.

Hundreds of dolphins emerged out of nowhere and began swimming alongside. I have a special place in my heart for dolphins, for they seem to be the only creatures anywhere who appreciate my singing. I sang out as the graceful cetaceans knifed across the bow, obviously pleased with *Gigi*'s increased speed. I crawled beneath the bow pulpit, reached down, and patted one husky, scarred fellow as he darted across the bow. I stroked another and another, as many dolphins vied to be the next patted. I don't know if they appreciated my affection, or if they were teasing me, but several large dolphins gave me a blast of spray right in the face. I let Ty oversleep as I enjoyed an unforgettable hour. On a sailboat the small events and the ocean's subtleties become very prominent.

Heavily laden, *Gigi* plodded south as the wind remained light for most of the first week. I had two nagging personal problems that I kept to myself. My left knee ached and actually popped like a cork coming out of a bottle of wine every time I straightened it. My mobility on deck was hampered, and I desperately hoped it would feel better before the weather turned nasty. (I had strained the knee riding in the back seat of a taxi. Rio's taxi drivers consider it a sport to see how close they can come to killing their passengers!) My second problem was Molly. I didn't anticipate the empty feeling her departure had left me with, although I have to admit, at times my memory is remarkably short. As I limped about the boat, I was constantly reminded of her by an article of clothing left behind or her handwriting in the log. I tried to block her out of my mind, but I was rarely successful.

As a diversion I thought more about our race with history. Our smart passage from Antigua to Rio de Janeiro had made up much of the time lost during the capsize and subsequent detour. With luck, we still had a chance to reach San Francisco in 120 sailing days. As *Gigi* sailed south on January 9, I calculated a few comparisons. An average 120-day clipper ship passage broke down into five parts: New York to the equator — 30 days; equator to 50° south — 26 days; 50° south to 50° south — 16 days; 50° south to equator — 23 days; equator to San Francisco — 25 days; 120 days total.

It is important to remember that the 120-day figure is strictly a rough average. In 1851, for example, *Flying Cloud* established her record run of just less than 90 days, but in that same year, the clippers *Cornwallis, Arthur,* and *Henry Allen* all needed more than 200 days to reach the Golden Gate.

By dividing our voyage into four legs, we sailed a longer and slower route than our historic rivals, who generally sailed nonstop. For this reason, we weren't overly burdened with guilt about using our diesel. Our maximum range under power was still less than the considerable distance added to our course by making landfalls in Bermuda, Rio de Janeiro and Valparaiso. Still, *Gigi* reached the equator in 35 sailing days, just five days behind schedule, and we were right on pace for a 25- or 26-day run to the 50th parallel.

As I sat sweating in the cabin on January 10, it was difficult to fathom that in less than 300 miles we would cross the ominous, red dotted line on the pilot chart, marking the extreme limit of icebergs. However, later that afternoon when I dove over the side to check the impeller on the speedometer, the possibility of an iceberg was easier to accept; the water was shockingly cold. Ty filmed my escapade and laughed as I balked at entering the frigid water. I completed my underwater repairs very quickly, and when I dragged myself back aboard he remarked, "I'm surprised you even got wet."

It was a constant challenge to keep *Gigi* moving in light air. We flew spinnakers when we could, poled out the genoa at every opportunity, and experimented with the staysail, sailing *Gigi* as a cutter — always in pursuit of that extra half knot of speed. Our labors were rewarded when I totaled up the first week's mileage and found that we'd averaged 118 miles per day.

On Friday the 13th, we drifted into iceberg territory. Icebergs and their smaller, more dangerous castaways, growlers and bergy bits, have posed a serious threat to navigation for mariners from all ages. Imagine a 300-foot clipper ship charging along at 15 knots with all sails flying, even the moonsails, and then suddenly crashing into a partially submerged growler! What a surprise that must have been. Ty and I wondered whether icebergs read pilot charts; we were both attentive on watch in our efforts to avoid any such surprises.

The next night I called Molly on the SSB. It was therapeutic for me just to hear her voice. However, she had awful news for us. Mike Kane and his crew had been forced to abandon ship when *Crusader* was dismasted south of Cape Horn. Fortunately, they were unharmed and quickly rescued by the Chilean Coast Guard. Ty and I reacted to the tragic news quite differently. I never viewed Mike Kane or Chay Blyth as competitors, and I was horrified to learn of Kane's misfortune. Ty, on the other hand, seemed pleased that *Crusader* was out of the picture.

"It's too bad," he remarked, "but it will make for a better story."

"Story," I lashed out at him. "Christ, Ty, think of other sailors out there somewhere, fighting for their lives in a life raft. Who gives a damn about the story!"

I cooled down after dinner, and on the midnight watch I reflected on what unlikely shipmates Ty and I are. Aside from offshore voyaging, we have few common interests, and we view the world from different perspectives. Yet, aboard *Gigi,* we get along surprisingly well. We have occasional angry outbursts, but in the confined world of a small sailboat it's vital to air your innermost feelings and not harbor deep grudges. You cannot escape confronting your shipmate in a 32-by-9-foot world, and invariably your true feelings must come to the surface. The sea is our common bond, and Ty and I both have an intense desire to sail the oceans of our planet.

We maintained a couple of hundred miles of sea room off the coast of Argentina. South of the Rio de la Plata, the broad estuary that feeds the major seaports of Montevideo and Buenos Aires, the weather turned decisively cooler. It was time for a tactical decision. We had two choices for the approach to Cape Horn, the inshore or the offshore route. According to the pilot chart, if we closed the coast and ran inshore we would be assisted by a favorable current. However, *Ocean Passages for the World,* a British Admiralty publication, warned of light, fickle winds except during "pamperos."

The mere thought of a pampero frightened me. Spawned high in the Andes, pamperos are vicious, localized wind storms that sweep down out of the mountains and gather speed over the low-lying pampas region — hence the name. When the cold storms collide with the warm sea breezes, the result is often hurricane-force winds. Pamperos are generally short-lived, isolated, and a unique feature of the Argentine coast. Still, they can be destructive.

The offshore alternative, which bucked the stiff Falkland Current and increased the possibility of icebergs, seemed preferable to the coastal pampero route. My hunch was to remain offshore, and I followed it.

Coastal sailors and landsmen often evoke the hackneyed phrase: "We steered by the stars." I hate to say it, but it's true; most steering is done by the compass these days. Indeed, I think if most sailors were forced to steer by the twinkling heavens above, they would sail around in circles. However, it is possible to steer by the stars on long passages, and, with just a few easy calculations from the *Nautical Almanac,* anybody can determine a "steering star."

The stars march across the sky in a westerly direction every night. Astronomers have recorded an imaginary ground position here on earth beneath every star for every second of every day. They record these positions in the annual *Nautical Almanac.* By matching the geographic coordinates of your destination with those of a bright star's ground point at a precise time each evening, you can ensure that that bright star is directly

*John taking a sun sight in
the Southern Ocean.*

over your destination. If you were to take a compass bearing on the star, that bearing would represent the most direct course to your destination. Unfortunately, this system, which was first devised by the Polynesians, is useful only when your destination is a considerable distance away. Otherwise your steering star will be too high in the sky to allow you to take a directional bearing.

We were lucky during the passage south to have Canopus, the second brightest star in the sky, as our steering star. Each night around 2300 Canopus would pass over a point directly above Le Maire Strait, allowing us to check our heading.

All this talk of stars may seem obsolete with the dawning of electronic navigation. Even line-of-position celestial navigation is a dying art. I suppose the sextant is an evolutionary dinosaur compared to an instantaneous, talking SatNav, but it seems a pity to me. Celestial navigation is more than just finding your way across an ocean, it's a communion with nature. I have spent hours studying the sky, waiting for a brief glimpse of the sun. Landfalls are imminently more gratifying when you've used the sun, moon, and stars to guide you. Do we really want to make offshore voyaging as effortless as possible? In the elimination of risks, do we also eliminate the rewards? I know that resistance to change is never the right tack, but at what point do we destroy the very purpose that has compelled us to take to the sea in the first place?

As *Gigi* sailed ever southward, shipping traffic virtually disappeared. Yet we were never alone. The sky was alive with seabirds. Magnificent wandering albatross soared on the wind currents, swift fulmers passed close by the masthead, and flittery stormy petrels struggled to remain airborne just above the surface of the sea. Watching a persistent stormy petrel fight its way upwind reminded me of what *Gigi* must look like to an observer on the celestial sphere as she clawed her way to windward.

After lunch on January 16, Ty mixed up our standard boat cocktail, gin and Tang, warm. We toasted our winged companions and took a swig. Ugh, salty. We looked at each other with wide eyes — obviously he had filled the glasses from the freshwater tanks. We dashed below to check the tanks. The 15-gallon bilge tank is fitted with a convenient inspection plate, which Ty promptly unscrewed before tasting the water; it was salty! Desperately we removed everything from the forepeak and checked the bladder tank in the bow. Its precious contents were also contaminated by salt water. In all, almost 30 gallons of drinking water were destroyed.

After the shock passed, we sat down and rationally discussed the situation. "Well, Ty, let's not overreact. Things are not that grim. Let's see, we still have 12 gallons in jerry jugs and about 10 gallons in plastic bottles." I walked to the chart table and quickly estimated the distance to Valparaiso. "It's about 1,200 miles down to the Horn and roughly 1,800 miles up the coast in the Pacific; 3,000 miles in all. If we can average 100 miles a day, we will need 30 days, and we have about 22 gallons of water. Heck, that's more than two-thirds of a gallon a day between us."

I tried to sound optimistic, but Ty wasn't buying my logic.

He stood beside me and studied the chart.

"I think we should make port in either Argentina or the Falkland Islands and replenish our supply. It will only take 62 hours at the most. Come on, John, look at it sensibly. It may take 30 days just to get around the Horn."

"But don't forget, Ty, if things become desperate we have an emergency desalinator."

"Yes, I know, but according to the brochure it produces a quart of drinking water after two hours of hard pumping! And we don't even know if it works."

Ty's reasoning was sound; once we were farther south off the desolate Patagonian coast, safe harbors were few and far between. "Let's head to Port Stanley in the Falklands," Ty suggested.

"Ty, this is going to sound brash, but for more than three months I have been fighting to get within striking distance of Cape Horn. Because of our numerous delays we are already late in the season, and we both know that a stop always kills at least a week. Ty, my hunch is to press on. We'll ration our water and closely monitor our consumption. If things become critical, we can duck into the Straits of Magellan. For now, let's keep going."

Ty was not pleased with my decision, but he was wise enough not to dispute it and throw our little power structure out of balance. After all, a captain has to be captain.

The following day, Ty discovered how the tanks had been contaminated in the first place. Contessa, for some unknown reason, mounted the water filler caps on the low deck, amidships. Every time *Gigi* heeled to port, the caps were completely submerged. The caps were plastic, a supposedly new innovation replacing the normal bronze caps that tend to corrode. However, the cold weather and water caused the plastic caps to contract and, consequently, to leak. We solved the problem by plugging up the filler hoses from down below, but unfortunately, it was a day too late to save our drinking water.

I was ornery and hard to live with as we sailed south. South, south, south. I felt condemned to sail south forever. I longed to turn the corner and round Cape Horn, and then head north. In spite of my somber moods, Ty and I were doing a fine job of keeping ahead of the ship. Every morning we made a list of daily chores and we attacked every problem with vigor. I abandoned my motto of, "If it's broken, figure out how you don't need it anymore," in favor of the old Boy Scout credo, "Be prepared."

On January 18 we crossed the 40th parallel and officially entered the "roaring forties." The forties don't roar in the Atlantic as they do in the Pacific, but still, once in the forties we felt like mountaineers who had finally reached the actual slope after months in the foothills. I wanted to share the Southern Ocean experience with Molly, and I wrote her long letters in my journal. I missed her in many ways. I wanted her to rub my neck and assure me that I was up to the demanding task ahead. I wanted her to explain the migratory patterns of seabirds. I wanted her eagle eyes to scan the horizon at night. I guess I just wanted her. I realized, or just remembered, that life at sea is quickly reduced to basics, and Molly is basic to my happiness.

I'd like to blame it on the Southern Ocean — that lonely region of wind and waves can affect your mind in unpredictable ways — but the truth is, as far as anyone can be sure, I was of sound mind when I tried to call Molly on SSB on the night of January 18. I had made up my mind to propose to her. I wrote out a list of important things I wanted to say and patched through the call.

Luckily, the transmission was clear, and the operator in Miami dialed Molly's number in Texas. Her phone rang once. I was as nervous as a schoolboy asking a cheerleader out for a date. Then the phone rang again. Then it rang a third, fourth, and fifth time. It continued to ring until the operator came on and said, "I'm sorry, sir, but nobody is home. Would you like to try another number?" I was devastated. I was all set to sweep Molly off her feet, and convince her to come to Chile and marry me. "Um, well, yes, I'll place another call." I called my brother, Tom, in Michigan. I just couldn't risk not letting somebody know of my intentions; what if we were unable to transmit in the future? Tom was delighted to hear from me.

"Tommy, I have an important message for you," I shouted. It was always necessary to shout into the microphone to be heard over the diesel which we ran while transmitting to keep the batteries charged. "Would you please call Molly in Texas and tell her that I want her to come to Chile and marry me. Tell her to set up everything and plan to arrive between February 10th and 20th, 1984."

"John," Tom responded incredulously, "are you asking me to propose for you?"

"Yes, I guess I am. I am not sure that we will be able to get calls through in the future; the transmissions have been pretty sketchy lately."

"OK, John, I'll call her. By the way, how are you doing and what is your position?"

"We are about 1,000 miles north of the Horn. It's damn cold and we are a little short of water, but otherwise we're OK."

I had done it — well, sort of. It never occurred to me that Molly wouldn't be as excited as I was. Just knowing that she would be in Valparaiso waiting for me sent my confidence soaring like a high flying albatross.

The following night I tried to reach Molly again, and this time I got through to her. Tommy had done his job but Molly was quite confused. I confirmed Tommy's story, of which she was suspect, and told her how much our love meant to me. "Well, you are lucky that I love you so damn much, Johnny, because that was the craziest proposal I've ever heard of." She assured me that she would be in Chile to meet us and take care of all the wedding details. I am a very fortunate man to have her for a partner.

We experienced the sudden fury of a pampero on January 21, despite our margin of sea room. The light of dawn was swallowed up by a huge black cloud that produced vicious, 50-knot gusts. Ty was on watch, and he slapped two deep reefs in the main and rolled in most of the headsail, and *Gigi* held her course. It is hard to imagine a better sea-boat, of any length; *Gigi* excells when most yachts are ready to seek shelter.

Later that same morning we were becalmed. We shook out the reefs in the main and I went forward to hoist the spinnaker. Stupidly, I hoisted the pole on the topping lift before I had all the lines arranged, and, as *Gigi* rolled in the swells, the pole swung first outboard and then back inboard, clobbering me on the side of the head. I was knocked off my feet and felt dizzy. We decided to forget the spinnaker and just rolled out the genoa. In the morning I had a lump on my temple the size of a golf ball.

A sailboat is much like the wind that propels her. She can travel thousands of miles, riding along the ocean's outer edge, but she leaves no record of her passing. She leaves no footprints on the surface of the sea once her wake is assimilated astern, and her course is always ahead, never behind. However, the ocean floor tells another tale.

Sailing between the Falkland Islands and the coast of Argentina, I couldn't help but think of the sailors buried beneath me. Young men, like myself, senseless victims of nationalistic pride, lay scattered among the rocks and sand, 10,000 feet below; footprints of man's insanity.

Albatross soared above and the steel blue ocean looked primeval. It was hard to imagine that desolate region of Earth filled with battleships and aircraft carriers. Yet, a year before, war had raged; pride had been at stake. From the perspective of our tiny, 32-foot world, the absurdity of war sang out from every wave.

8

Cape Horn to Starboard

*A*CCORDING TO MY DEAD reckoning, a mess of intersecting lines and columns sprawled across a saturated plotting sheet, *Gigi* crossed the 50th parallel in the South Atlantic at 1000 hours on January 25, 1984. There should have been a bold line of demarcation stretched across the water, but there wasn't. *Gigi* was surrounded by the same steely blue Atlantic Ocean that she had been sailing over for 7,000 miles. The setting was deceptively serene as a few meandering rays of sunshine pierced the cloud layer and cast a glow upon the sea. We weren't fooled, however. In our minds there was no mistaking it; our assault on Cape Horn had just begun.

Throughout the story I've spoken in terms of "doubling Cape Horn." Author and sailing ship master, Alan Villiers, defines the somewhat confusing phrase in his classic volume *The Way of a Ship*.

> *"Sailors in the sailing ship era, when they spoke of rounding the Horn, meant to sail westward from the latitude of 50 south in the Atlantic, down around Cape Horn up to 50 in the Pacific; nothing else was counted as a Cape Horn rounding, for the eastward passage before the westerly gales was reckoned no rounding at all. The distance a sailing ship had to travel to get from 50 south to 50 south past the Horn was at least 1,200 miles — every mile of it invariably a bitter fight."*

Ty and I were actually relieved to finally be in the infamous waters close to the Horn. We were both thirsting for our first taste of a legendary Cape Horn "snorter." I think we both wanted to know if we could endure a Southern Ocean storm while there was still a chance to turn back. For centuries mariners have cursed the Horn and then praised it in the same sentence. The Horn has lured deepwater sailors as though it was a holy shrine, and a yachting journey to Cape Horn today is surely a personal pilgrimage, for you must hear the call of the Horn from deep within. There is no other sensible reason to venture south below 50°.

On January 26, when Ty came below to rouse me after his early morning watch, he was stunned to find himself standing in 6 inches of water. "Let's go, John, get up. It looks like we have a bit of a problem." Ty hustled back into the cockpit to pump the bilge, and I pulled on my seaboots and heavy sweater. We didn't panic, because we were accustomed to hardships, and a leak was just another hardship.

"Where is the water coming from?" I repeated to myself as I tried to think logically.

I checked the seacocks in the head, a usual leak point, but they were both closed. I checked all other through-hull fittings and the stuffing box where the prop shaft exits the hull, but I still couldn't find the source of the leak. Ty finally sucked the pump dry after 350 strokes, and collapsed into bed. "I'll stay ahead of the water and keep searching for the leak," I said as I climbed into the cockpit.

Leaving the cabin was always a shocking experience in the high southern latitudes. The temperature hovered at 40°F and I huddled beneath the spray dodger as *Gigi* drove into a rising southwest wind. I made a mental list of possible leak sources: ports, exhaust backup, hull damage.

"No, I won't even consider hull damage," I said aloud. "Please, not now, not when we're this close to the Horn. Please make it something simple," I pleaded to the ocean.

Gigi was heeled hard to port, and I noticed a lot of standing water on the low-side cockpit seat. I thought to myself, "The draining channels from the seat to the cockpit scuppers must be clogged," when the water suddenly disappeared. Several times I watched a wave slop aboard, and after a few seconds the standing water would disappear all at once. I flung open the sail locker beneath the seat and carefully examined the gasket. It was loose because of a gaping tear, and the mysterious water was obviously flooding into the locker beneath the seat. I then followed the path of the water and was horrified to learn that it drained into the cabin along the side of the hull, down through the galley lockers, and finally into the bilge. However, with *Gigi* heeled hard to port, most of the water drained straight onto the cabin sole!

When Ty woke up, I told him I had found the leak. We scoured the boat for thick rubber gasket material, but it was one of the few spares we didn't have aboard. I resorted to indispensable duct tape and fashioned a makeshift repair of the old gasket. Ty undertook the delicate job of enlarging the drainhole into the bilge. He had to drill through half-inch teak with a rusty hand drill, and there was just a quarter inch of clearance above the hull. Fortunately, our repairs succeeded in stopping most of the water from coming below, and the water that did find its way below was channeled into the bilge.

The winds shifted to the southeast in the afternoon and I was disgusted. "Why southeast winds now?" I complained to Ty. "Couldn't they have waited a few more days when we would need to go west? The chance of southeast winds off Cape Horn are one in a hundred." Methodically, we checked off every chore on our 50 south project list, except one. We delayed bending on our heavy-weather sails. Frequently, we needed more headsail than a standard working jib, and with the Harken roller-furling system performing well, I decided to leave the genoa set. Alan Villiers, no doubt, influenced my decision when he wrote in *The Way of a Ship:*

> *"There is no doubt that the dread of the Horn had an effect on far too many masters. As soon as they neared 50 south in the Atlantic they shorted their ships down to wait for it. Of course, they got it then. If they had fought back, if they sailed (as many did) with quiet confidence born of courage and ability, then getting past the Horn was no worse than a winter rounding of Hatteras or Flattery, or a beat down channel against the November gales. The broad principles for getting around were well established. It was a fight, and a hard one. In the last analysis, it was the quality and endurance of the fighter which counted. Of course, the ship had to be good too."*

At 0200 on January 27, I called my brother, Tom, on the SSB. I had to call at that early hour because our radio waves propagated much farther in the darkness. I kidded him that it was too late for us to take the Straits of Magellan, as we were already south of Cape Virgins. Tom had recently spoken with Molly, and he told us she had been very busy. She had contacted the Argentine Navy and the Chilean Coast Guard and told them that we would soon be rounding Cape Horn. (It was reassuring to know that if we needed emergency assistance, somebody would be in the neighborhood and ready to render it.) Molly also contacted my mother in Tahiti, where she was aboard the *Epoch*. Mom wrote back saying she and Tim were coming to Chile for our wedding. Our wedding party was really taking shape. However, it seemed to me that the "groom to be" had the hard part. First, he had to negotiate the treacherous Le Maire Strait, then fight past Cape Horn, and, finally, claw his way nearly 2,000 miles up the most dangerous lee shore on the planet — What a man will do to get married!

Later that morning, the gray, lingering twilight played a nasty trick on me. I was below brewing up a pot of coffee when I had a premonition that something was wrong. I poked my head up through the companion-way and was shocked to see what appeared to be an iceberg off the port bow. I fetched the binoculars and studied the frozen derelict. It looked like a growler, low in the water and greenish-gray in color. I quickly tacked about, but as I hauled in on the jib sheet I noticed another growler dead ahead! Panicked, I frantically started to come about again when I spotted another growler behind me and another off to starboard. We were surrounded! Just then the sun emerged from behind a cloud and all the icebergs disappeared. I'd been terrorized by ice mirages, and I felt like a fool. My body trembled as I brought *Gigi* back on course.

A few hours later *Gigi* sailed into a thick fog bank. I considered sounding the fog horn, but finally decided that I'd only succeed in disturbing the albatross and waking Ty. As we glided silently southward, I could only estimate our noon position. According to my dead reckoning, we were at 53°50' south, and 65°15' west, or 50 miles due north of Le Maire Strait.

Le Maire Strait is a treacherous passage between the eastern shore of Tierra del Fuego and Staten Island. After the Pacific Ocean roars past Cape Horn, much of the water funnels northward through the 19-mile-long, 16-mile-wide strait. Strong, isolated tidal races and swift tidal streams ebb and flow through the strait, causing vicious seas when they oppose the wind and current. Marcell Bardiaux, a hearty Frenchman who spent eight years circumnavigating the world aboard his famous yawl, *Les 4 Vents,* was capsized twice as he tried to clear Le Maire Strait!

Why then did we choose Le Maire Strait over the longer but safer route east of Staten Island? Le Maire Strait represents a short-cut that makes the approach to Cape Horn more direct. It saves at least 100 sailing miles and possibly several days of beating south of Staten Island. Also, once through the strait, the offshore islands perched at the tip of the South American continent provide a nifty lee for the final approach to the Horn. Still, I have to admit, it was with a great deal of trepidation that I pointed *Gigi*'s bow toward Le Maire Strait.

I chose teriyaki steak for lunch. I know that sounds glamorous, but some of the glitz is lost when you consider that the steak was packaged in aluminum foil and boiled for only three minutes. Ty only resorted to foil-packaged lunches when the going was rough, or he was just not in the mood for cooking. The packaged meals made by Yurika Foods were delicious and gave us a much-needed variety in our diet. Because they could be boiled in salt water, we were able to preserve our precious fresh-water supply.

After lunch I sat at the chart table and formulated our plan of action. The wind had clocked around again and was blowing from the north-northeast, which allowed us to ease the sheets and romp south. The sailing directions for the east coast of South America recommend that vessels enter Le Maire Strait one hour after high tide. Unfortunately, the next high tide was at 0200 on January 28. I decided to sail south until 1900 hours or until we were about 25 miles above the strait. Then we would heave-to until midnight before setting sail again and begin cautiously creeping toward the strait. I hoped the early light of twilight would give us enough visibility to take bearings on Cape San Diego. It was a risky plan, but with a fair wind I was confident we could pull it off. However, shortly after we made our plans, the weather started to deteriorate. Weather changes abruptly in the Southern Ocean, and during the late afternoon and early evening of January 27, the barometer starting falling like a skydiver without a parachute.

By 1800 hours it was obvious we had to alter our plans. We hove-to approximately 30 miles north of Le Maire Strait as a full gale developed. Visibility became atrocious as icy rains accompanied the strengthening northeast winds. The barometer kept plunging. I recorded its decline in the log: 1200 hours — 1005 millibars; 1500 hours — 996 millibars; 1800 hours — 990 millibars; 2100 hours — 984 millibars. The Force 8 gale that engulfed us made the coast of Tierra del Fuego a potential lee shore. At 2300 hours I wrote in the log:

> *"It's too bad. It's too damn bad. It looks like we've missed everything by one day. This gale couldn't have come at a worse time. It looks like we'll have to sail back and forth tonight to maintain sea room and try and get through the strait with the tide at 1500 hours tomorrow. I'm thinking about going around Staten Island after all. The wind is steady at 35 knots, gusting to 45."*

By midnight the barometer had dropped to 973 millibars — a fall of 33 millibars in 12 hours. I expected *Gigi* to be swallowed up at any moment and never to be heard from again. In the northern hemisphere, 973 millibars, which equates to a reading of 28.7 inches, would almost surely indicate hurricane-force winds. Yet the monumental Cape Horn storm we expected never developed. In the morning, despite a barometric reading of 971 millibars, the winds moderated to a steady 30 knots. We decided to take advantage of the northeast winds and made sail for Le Maire Strait once again.

January 28 was possibly the most trying day of the entire voyage. It started off OK when Ty spotted the distant peaks of Staten Island off the port bow at 1100 hours. Our dead reckoning had been surprisingly accurate, considering I hadn't taken a sight in 36 hours. We adjusted our course toward the southwest and drove for Le Maire Strait. An hour later, Cape San Diego on the island of Tierra del Fuego, loomed into view. But Cape Horn seemed to be teasing us, taunting us, because the wind shifted abruptly to the south and Staten Island and Tierra del Fuego were quickly obscured by fog and mist.

Still we sailed on, determined to get through. At 1500 hours we entered what we hoped was about the center of Le Maire Strait. Visibility was down to a couple of boat lengths, and, for the first time in my life, I longed for a SatNav. All morning the northeast gale-force winds collided with a contrary tidal stream, creating dangerously steep seas. *Gigi* was viciously pitched about and twice knocked over almost 90 degrees. Ty and I had to hold on for dear life.

For two long hours we made short tacks, trying to con *Gigi* through the strait. We just couldn't make any progress against the head winds and cross seas. Finally, we conceded defeat and ran back to the north. "Fuck the Le Maire Strait," Ty hollered, and shook his fist toward the south.

"I always wanted to see Staten Island," I added, defeated, as *Gigi* sped northward.

I think the ghost of a proud clipper ship captain was reminding us that Cape Horn is not a place for amateurs. "OK, boys, let's test your mettle a bit." And test our mettle he did. As *Gigi* ran northward, the wind did the impossible; it shifted to the east and blew up to 50 knots. An easterly gale made the eastern tip of Staten Island a rare windward mark, and neither Ty nor I had the spirit to drive *Gigi* to windward all night long. I didn't know what to do. We just let the boat sail north, away from Cape Horn, away from Le Maire Strait, away from everything we'd been fighting for through four long months.

When we reckoned we had plenty of sea room, we hove-to under a triple-reefed main and staysail. During the night I scolded Ty for not keeping a proper lookout on his watch. It was a miserable night; it was 37 °F in the cabin and colder on deck. A driving rain virtually eliminated visibility.

"What do you expect me to see?" Ty asked.

I blew up. "I don't care if you can't see the end of your goddamned nose, get back up in the cockpit. Listen, Ty, we are really vulnerable when we are hove-to, and as long as there are two of us aboard, somebody's going to be looking about!" Reluctantly, Ty climbed into the cockpit. Whether or not he promptly went to sleep again is something only he knows. One thing I do know, the light of dawn was never more eagerly awaited.

At first light we tacked south. The gale had moderated and *Gigi* easily fended off the seas on a beam reach. My dead reckoning was almost illegible because my fingers were too cold to grip the pencil. We desperately needed a sun sight; just a brief glimpse of the sun would allow me to determine longitude. At 0730 the sun momentarily ducked out from behind a cloud. I dashed below and grabbed my sextant. Then I woke Ty, handed him the notebook to record the sights, and scurried back on deck. But the sun was gone. Three times I repeated this mad dashing about before I caught the sun and managed a few acceptable sights.

The LOP confirmed my dead-reckoning longitude, and according to dead-reckoning latitude, we were about 30 miles north of Le Maire Strait. The wind was still easterly, and it looked as though our timing to sneak through was just right. We sailed until noon and hove-to again, approximately 10 miles above Le Maire Strait.

"Ty," I said, as we sat in the cockpit, "I'm sorry about last night."

"So am I, let's forget it. What do you say we head for this damn strait one more time with reckless abandon!"

"Reckless abandon it is, my friend, but not before I cook lunch."

That produced a hearty laugh from Ty, but undaunted, I went below and cooked up a whopping batch of rubbery pancakes.

"Hey, there's the sun," Ty hollered. I dropped my spatula and grabbed my sextant. Wedging myself between the stern pulpit and the backstay, I waited until I had a clear view of the horizon. Then I rocked my sextant to make sure I'd measured the lowest point of the sun's reflected image and yelled, "Mark." Ty recorded the time and altitude, and we succeeded in obtaining four accurate sights.

As I started down the companionway steps, I was shocked. Then I started to laugh.

"What's so funny?" Ty asked.

"Look," I said pointing to the stove. The bowl of pancake batter had spilled, and an enormous pancake was frying on the stove top!

We were in for another shock when I reduced the sights and determined latitude. Current, leeway, and probably exhaustion had combined to put my dead-reckoning latitude in error by 30 miles. We weren't 10 miles above Le Maire Strait, we were 40! We would have to sail like *Australia II* to catch the tide at 1600. The weather finally sympathized with our plight as the wind clocked to the north and held steady at Force 7. We poled out the genoa and ran with a reefed main, wing and wing.

At 1430, Ty spotted the rugged peaks of Staten Island for the second time, nearly 48 hours later. The round top of Cape San Diego loomed into view an hour later. We took a series of running fixes and confirmed our position as we entered the Strait at 1630. I had been hand steering all afternoon, but not because the Navik wind vane wasn't up to the task; I just had an unbearable urge to drive *Gigi* through the strait.

Ironically, halfway through the strait, the wind died out. In a hurry to get through, we promptly cranked over the iron genny. The favorable tidal stream was whisking us along at 4 knots, and we surged out of Le Maire Strait making 9 knots over the bottom. As the light of January 30 receded into the twilight, the peaks of Staten Island faded from view astern. We had a clear shot at Cape Horn, 100 miles away to the southwest.

Cape Horn is actually an island, the southernmost of the Wollaston Islands. There is nothing west of Cabo de Hornos except uninterrupted ocean for 5,000 miles. Relentless westerly winds, named for their latitudes, the roaring forties and furious fifties, sweep across this vast fetch of open ocean unperturbed by land masses. As a result the seas build, and build, and keep building, until they either collide with the southwest coast of Chile or funnel between Cape Horn and the Antarctic peninsula 50 miles to the south. January 30 was our last night in the Atlantic Ocean — Cape Horn and the fury of the Pacific lay ahead.

The wind returned with a vengeance during the evening, but instead of continuing to clock to the west, it backed to the east. We were forced to harden the sheets as the Wollaston Islands became an unlikely lee shore. We held our course through the night, and in the morning the barometer started to soar. Although the weather remained cold and blustery, it boosted our confidence to watch the needle swing to the right.

At 1000 on January 31, I spotted Barnevelt Island dead ahead. We pinched up to 30° off the apparent wind to avoid tacking. At noon Cape Horn loomed into view off the starboard beam. We eased the sheets and steered a course to pass close aboard. At 1500 *Gigi* was three miles due south of Cape Horn.

The Horn was a sight I'll never forget. Cape Horn is not beautiful — it's humbling. It's a brazen, rocky headland that has somehow defied the

Cape Horn off the starboard bow.

ravages of erosion. It jauntily juts its craggy chin into the cold blue sea, dividing the two great oceans of our planet. Ty and I didn't whoop and yell, we marveled. I remembered the words of Jim Whittaker, the first American to reach the summit of Mt. Everest: "You don't conquer a mountain like this, you conquer yourself." I suddenly understood. I understood that you don't assault or conquer Cape Horn, and you don't boast about being the first this or the smallest that. I tried to picture the scene from a vantage point in the sky, and I had to laugh because the view seemed almost quaint. An absurdly small yacht with flags flying astern, two men from the Midwest with less than 10 years sailing experience between them, and, to the north, frowning Cape Horn. I remembered a young boy and a young girl floundering about in a plastic dinghy in the Florida Keys four years before. Hal Roth, a Cape Horn veteran, wrote that "a voyage around Cape Horn is a trip to the ultimate classroom of the sea." Cape Horn was the pinnacle of my sailing apprenticeship, maybe. I was finally ready to call myself a sailor, maybe.

The benevolent east wind blew into a full gale as we skirted the

Horn, heading due west. For the first time in 7,500 miles and 70 sailing days, *Gigi* was bound west and then north. At 1700 hours our last glimpse of the Horn was obscured, as the thick clouds reached down to the sea. We charged into the Pacific Ocean with a reefed main and 100 percent genoa.

During the night of January 31, the wind shifted to the northwest. I was strangely comforted by the prevailing northwest head winds; the easterlies had left me feeling guilty. At noon on February 1, I totaled up 148 miles — our best run of Leg II. However, in many respects the difficult aspects of Leg II were just beginning.

Glancing at a chart of the southern coast of Chile, you can quickly

Ty raising the signal flags off Cape Horn.

determine the direction of the prevailing winds: westerly. For more than 1,000 miles the coast has been savagely eroded. The maze of islands and rocks that guard the coast are an almost impenetrable lee shore. It's paramount to maintain sufficient sea room as you fight your way north, battling westerly gales.

On the night of February 1, I reached WOM in Miami, and they patched a call through to Molly in Texas. She sighed with relief when I told her we were safely around Cape Horn. She told me that the Argentine Navy had contacted her, requesting our position, three days ago. Because of the catastrophic drop in atmospheric pressure, hurricane-force winds had been predicted, and they were planning an air-and-sea search for us. But we never saw a ship, or plane, or conditions that we couldn't handle. Fate had smiled on us.

Molly also gave us more details of Mike Kane's misfortune. He had already rounded Cape Horn and reportedly was a couple of days ahead of record pace when a shackle on his backstay parted. Before the crew could do anything, the mast tumbled to the deck, and their hopes for beating *Flying Cloud*'s record were dashed. They cut away the rig and triggered their Argos satellite transmitter. The Chilean Coast Guard quickly came to the rescue, but *Crusader,* the first trimaran to round Cape Horn from east to west, was abandoned.

I assured Molly that I loved her and I had just put the finishing touches on a song that I was writing for her and for our wedding. She made me promise that I would recite it, not sing it, and I reluctantly agreed.

On the 2300 to 0200 watch, I thought about *Crusader*. I wondered why the crew didn't try to effect a jury rig and at least make a stab at saving the boat. They could possibly have run back around the Horn and ducked into the Wollaston Islands or pressed on to Port Stanley in the Falkland Islands. It's impossible to judge another sailor's actions, and, to be sure, I didn't know the extent of the damage or the morale of the crew. Still, I wondered, if they hadn't had an Argos transmitter, would they have saved their boat out of necessity?

We spent most of February 2 becalmed! Becalmed at 56° S, 74° W, an area where the pilot chart forecasts a gale one day in five, and usually Force 6 conditions. We took advantage of the respite and attended to several chores. We cleaned the battery terminals, chipped the corrosion from the electrical switches, and tidied up the cabin.

We managed to drift 61 miles February 3, and the wind finally returned in the afternoon. We decided not to engage the diesel unless it was an absolute emergency. A problem had developed with the transmis-

Ty catches up on his reading in fair weather.

sion, and the little Yanmar thumped violently whenever we put it in gear. Also, the lee shore, 100 miles to the east, was never far from my mind, and I wanted to conserve every drop of fuel in case we had to claw our way offshore.

Our luck continued though, as the wind came up from the south. Ty insisted it was because I finally proposed to Molly after five years of living in sin. "That's hogwash," I exclaimed. But for whatever reason, the cold blast of air off the Antarctic peninsula pushed *Gigi* steadily northward. *Gigi*'s direct track around the Horn was a stark contrast to the legendary beat of the *Edward Sewall* in 1914. One of the last commercial squareriggers, the *Sewall* needed 67 days to beat around the Horn from 50° south to 50° south. She encountered almost two months of gale-force westerlies, and her track chart from 50 to 50 looked like a three-year-old's creation on an Etch-A-Sketch. Three times she was well around the Horn before gales drove her back to the east. Captain Richard Quick, certainly a misnomer, was a Cape Horn veteran. He

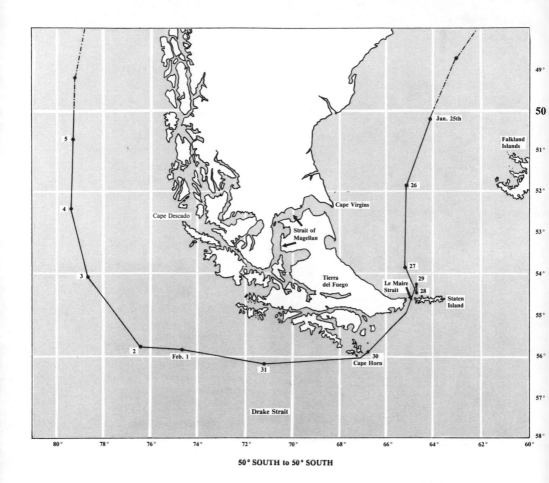

50° SOUTH to 50° SOUTH

refused to give in, and when the *Sewall* finally fetched Honolulu, she was 263 days out of Philadelphia.

The southerly winds lost their steam as we sailed into a pocket of high pressure. On February 4, we were nearly becalmed once again, on the same parallel as Cape Desire. The sails slatted as *Gigi* bobbed on swells spawned in New Zealand. Ty cooked up an enormous batch of my favorite Romanian beef stew. We had a Bloody Mary before lunch, and a few tangoes with the stew. Afterward, we had several more tangoes with dessert.

I told Ty about Sir Francis Drake, who, 400 years before us, encountered a monumental gale not far from where we sat becalmed. Drake, aboard the *Golden Hind,* survived, but his sister ship, *Marigold,* was lost with all hands. I also told Ty about Joshua Slocum. He, too, encountered a fierce gale as he cleared Cape Desire in his famous yawl, *Spray. Spray* was driven almost all the way back to Cape Horn before she eluded the tempest after a harrowing passage through the Milky Way, a rock-strewn passage between the Drake Strait and Magellan Strait.

Ty became pensive after I finished my sea stories, and the calm lingered.

"John, I love it out here," he said, "but differently than you do. I'm not into the history of this or that. I really don't care much for the past. I like the solitude of the sea. I'm a very lonely man, as you know, but out here . . . . Well, it's difficult to explain. I guess it may sound strange, but out here I'm never lonely.

"I've made certain choices in my life, and I'll tell you truthfully, at times I hate the world back there. I'm weary of business, and the only reason I keep at it is because I have a commitment to my family. My wife," he paused, searching for the right words, "well, let me put it this way. I don't write songs about her. I respect her and I need her, but we don't have much affection between us anymore. I love my two boys, and Gigi does a good job with them. I'm sure, in many ways, I am a stranger to them.

"You have Molly, John. Love her, John. Love her every day. I know that I exasperate you sometimes, and we have our differences, but I count you as my friend."

I didn't know what to say, or maybe I did. I just didn't know how to say it. I smiled at Ty and said, "We've battled the English Channel, we've crossed the Atlantic, and we've rounded Cape Horn. We've been through a hell of a lot together, Ty. You've been a friend, and a father, and given me a lot of opportunities. Thank you!"

In the morning the wind shifted to the north-northwest and once again blew into a gale. But nothing could stop us then. We shortened the sails and drove on. Before midnight, according to my dead reckoning, we crossed the 50th parallel in the Pacific. We doubled Cape Horn in 11½ days, faster than any yacht had before. It seemed as if San Francisco was just around the bend.

9

Rendezvous in Valparaiso

A SAILOR SHOULD NEVER prematurely dream about the end of a voyage. Although the furious fifties had been surprisingly feeble, the notorious roaring forties seemed determined to live up to their reputation. I was still feeling the effects of the previous night's festivities when Ty tapped me on the shoulder for the 0200 watch. The sobering, cold northwest winds that greeted me in the cockpit banished any thoughts of San Francisco from my mind. We still had more than 1,000 miles to Valparaiso.

At 0500 I tapped Ty's shoulder without remorse, quickly stripped off my layers of foul-weather gear and pile clothing, and took his place in the warm bunk. We "hot bunked," shared a berth, the entire voyage, because the cabin was crammed with gear. When *Gigi* was heeled precariously and plunging into steep seas, sleeping was always a challenge. It was essential to find a position of equilibrium, wedged up against the saloon table, which served as a leeboard.

I had just entered the realm of fantasy land, that blissful state when you really don't give a damn about the boat anymore. I was vividly dreaming about walking on a beach with Molly. Her tanned, naked body was pressed against me, and her golden hair was blowing in the wind. I could taste her lips as we stopped to kiss, when, suddenly, *Gigi* smashed into a freight train. The saloon table exploded out of the floor and flew across the cabin. I followed in close pursuit and smashed my aching head on the leeward port. Luckily, I didn't break either the port or my head, but it surely was a rude awakening.

Ty hustled below and told me that the train was really a nasty cross sea that had knocked *Gigi* almost flat. The table I was resting against had been bolted to the floor with 4-inch studs, but the force of the wave had pulled the bolts right through the teak sole. We promptly propped the table back into place and lashed it to the handrails. We switched our sleeping berth to the starboard side, where the berth is only 5½-feet long, and wrung out the sopped sleeping bag. Despite a short bunk and soaked bedding, I promptly rejoined Molly on the beach.

We pounded out 88 miles by noon on February 6, as the gale intensified. Taking accurate sights from *Gigi*'s pitching deck was a frustrating job. I would wedge myself between the cockpit coaming and the backstay and gingerly lower the sun's reflected image down to the horizon. Because of *Gigi*'s low freeboard, it was difficult to discern the actual horizon from the swell. Also, almost invariably, I would get doused by spray before I was satisfied with my sights, and then I had to rinse my sextant with fresh water and start again.

Speaking of fresh water, our modest drinking supply was holding out better than we expected. In the cold temperatures we drank much less water than we normally did, and our allotment of one quart each per day was sufficient. However, on February 7, another problem developed when both stove-top burners clogged up once again. Ty carefully took the burners apart and thoroughly soaked each fitting in kerosene. Then he confidently put the stove back together and asked me what I wanted for lunch. I ended up with cold tuna, because the burners had finally clogged up for good; they were beyond repair. Ty was able to light the oven burner after much pampering, and the sickly greenish flame at least let us heat coffee in the morning.

Despite this handicap, Ty managed to keep my belly full. My appetite aboard is voracious, while he, in contrast, eats rather sparingly. He was a bit chubby when we cleared Guanabara Bay, 30 days before. But as we neared Valparaiso, he was probably 20 pounds lighter and as hard as a rock.

The northwest gale persisted all day and the ride remained brutal. The SSB was our link with the outside world, an almost unreal world to us. I called Molly on February 8. I told her that we were just 800 miles away from our rendezvous, and our ETA was February 15. She was cheerful and told us that she had hotel reservations and five huge duffle bags full of spares and provisions to bring with her. She also confirmed that Mom and Tim were definitely coming as well. I was beaming after I hung up the microphone. My weekly chats with Molly gave me spirit to tackle anything.

The gale petered out the next day and the barometer started to soar. However, by noon on February 10, the barometer had done a rapid about-face and was spiraling downward. Later that night the wind shifted to the south, and we felt the first zephyrs of what was to become a Force 11 gale.

The waves anticipated the wind, and a long swell emerged from the south. During the morning of February 11 the storm racing northward from Antarctica caught up to us, and no wonder — it was blowing 60 knots! The seas accompanying the gale quickly developed into mountainous, breaking walls of water. Sailors routinely exaggerate the size of waves, but I can say with all honesty that some of the cresting combers piling up astern were at least 40 feet high!

Strangely, we found the wild roller-coaster ride exhilarating, not frightening. As a huge following sea overran us, *Gigi* would dig her heels into the wave and surge forward as though she'd been shot out of a cannon. We lowered the main and lashed the boom to the deck. We rolled in all but about 70 percent of the headsail and ran with speed. Unfortunately, our speedometer had packed it in earlier, so we could only estimate our speed. I swear, at times we must have hit 12 to 14 knots. It was necessary to hand steer and we took turns muscling the tiller. The unique beauty of the Southern Ocean's fury is impossible to describe. We were two sailors on a seaworthy boat, 35 days out from our last port — in harmony with the sea. In retrospect, our tactics may seem reckless, but we were guided by our instincts. Only in the Southern Ocean can the sun suddenly emerge from the seemingly impenetrable cloud cover of a Force 11 storm, and cast a halo over the entire scene.

Finally the euphoria faded as the tempest raged into the night. Steering became exhausting and the cold penetrated to the bone. We rolled in the rest of the headsail, and I inched forward on my fanny to set the staysail. As I hanked the sail to the stay, *Gigi* was swamped by a cascading wave. Rushing water swept me into the netting along the lifelines. I came up laughing and hollered at Ty, "Watch what you are doing." Then I noticed that the lanyard on my safety harness was not secured to anything. Clearly, it was time to get serious. My potential accident accentuated the importance of roller-furling headsails. If our staysail had been a roller-furling sail, I would never have been on the foredeck in those wild conditions.

With just the tiny staysail for locomotion, our speed slowed dramatically. The Navik wind vane took the helm, and by noon on February 12, the storm had moderated into a fine sailing breeze. When I calculated our latitude, I found that amazingly, the mighty storm had ushered us out of the roaring forties. At 37°43′ S, we were just a couple of days out of Valparaiso.

We spent most of the daylight hours of February 14 cleaning up the boat. We scrubbed the head and washed the floors. Ty cleaned the galley and I organized the cockpit. *Gigi* emerged from her ordeal with the Southern Ocean in remarkable condition. I also received a little grooming myself as Ty and I combined to give me a shave. "This is like trimming a hedge with dull scissors," Ty said as he cut away the bulk of my leathery beard. By the time I gave my poor face the final going-over with a razor, I was a bloody mess. Ty assured me that I would regret having a beard in my wedding pictures 10 years from then, but as I stared at the clean-shaven image in the mirror, I didn't recognize myself.

We closed the coast during the night. I wrote a letter to Molly in my journal.

> *"My lover, I'm looking for you ahead, somewhere beyond the bow. It's raining and* Gigi *slices silently through the water, searching for the guiding lights of Point Curanmilla and Point Angelus. They lie 30 tantalizing miles ahead. Even after all of these miles, landfalls are never easy.*
>
> *"It's hard to believe, baby, Cape Horn lies almost 1,600 miles astern. THE HORN — for so long the object of my dreams, my quixotic obsession, THE HORN — is a dream accomplished. So many of my dreams have slipped through my fingers, but not this one. Thanks for understanding my madness, and thanks for having the strength to let me try."*

At first light on February 15, we fixed our position with a running fix on Point Curanmilla. We skirted the rocky promontory on a reach, and cut Point Angelus as close as we dared. Once around the point, we spotted the breakwall protecting Valparaiso's inner harbor. Thirty-eight days and 4,200 miles out of Rio de Janeiro, I closed the logbook for Leg II.

The harbor was congested by several World War II–vintage destroyers. We raised the Port Captain on the VHF radio, and he instructed us to stay where we were; he was sending a launch to escort us to the Coast Guard dock. Within minutes, a blue and orange cutter steamed alongside and gestured for us to follow. We rafted alongside another Coast Guard vessel, and several sailors eagerly tended our lines. Strange-

LEG II
Rio de Janeiro, Brazil to Valparaiso, Chile

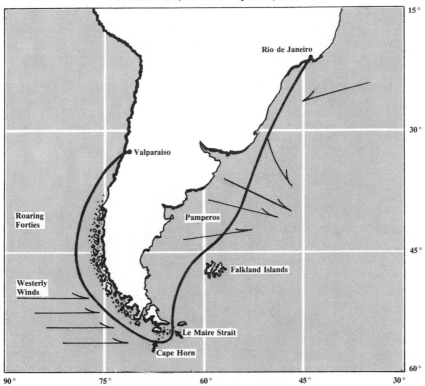

ly, several hundred people lined the quay, curiously examining us "Norte Americanos locos," in a most "pequeno barco."

Before *Gigi* was even secure, a reporter and a photographer leaped aboard. The reporter fired numerous questions at us in Spanish, and the photographer directed us all over the boat, posing for pictures. Soon, however, a Coast Guard officer arrived, shooed them away, and led us into the dreary, gray customs building. We cleared customs with surprising ease. The Port Captain, Patrico Gonzales, spoke excellent English. He was eager to hear about our passage around Cape Horn; he seemed truly awed by *Gigi*'s diminutive stature. He also told us that the last storm we encountered was a legitimate Force 11 — 55 to 63 knots! A coastal steamer had been lost during the storm, and I don't think he believed us when we told him we easily handled the tempest. He also gave us details of Mike Kane's dramatic rescue. He seemed slightly put out that Kane had tried to tell the captain of the rescue vessel how to come alongside his stricken craft.

The Port Captain recommended that we moor *Gigi* at the yacht club in Con Con, about 10 miles up the coast. The last thing Ty and I wanted to do was to climb back aboard *Gigi,* but after we filled a jerry jug with diesel fuel, that's just what we did. We motorsailed up the coast and negotiated a fierce tidal stream at the entrance to the Club Pacifico.

We moored *Gigi* bow-to. The club director, an expatriated German fellow, was offended when we offered to pay for dockage. "You will stay as guests of the club, I insist. Don't worry, your boat will be quite safe here. Now, gentlemen, if you don't mind me saying this, if I were you, I would take a taxi into town, check into a hotel, and take a very long and very hot shower!" He had read our minds, or possibly he was just standing downwind of us.

I was dying to find Molly. During our last radio conversation she told us that she had reservations at the Hotel O'Higgins. "Are you sure she said O'Higgins?" Ty asked me for the twentieth time.

"I know that sounds awfully Irish for Chile, but I am sure that's what she said."

The Hotel O'Higgins turned out to be a lovely inn in the heart of Vina del Mar. We later learned that Bernado O'Higgins is revered in Chile. He was the leader of Chile's War of Independence in 1810, and is known as the father of the country.

I was disappointed when the clerk informed me that Molly and Oz had not yet checked in. Ty and I went ahead and reserved our rooms and took the club director's advice. I let the scorchingly hot water beat down upon my battered body. After all, 38 days is quite a spell to go without a shower. Afterward, feeling squeaky clean, I lay down for a nap. I found the bed uncomfortably stationary, and after a few minutes of tossing and turning, I went down to the cafe to wait for Molly.

No sooner had I ordered a bottle of the house white, than Molly came bounding into the lobby. I yelled to her, and she changed course without slowing down. She leaped into my arms. "You did it, baby. You did it!" she cried, in between kisses. Then she put her hand on my face. "Whew, whew, smooooth. I know what's on your mind." I laughed and kissed her again and again.

Oz and Ty joined us in the cafe and we talked excitedly about the passage behind and the passage ahead. I couldn't take my eyes off Molly, and I clutched her hand as though someone might try to snatch her away from me. Along with another bottle of wine, our waiter brought a copy of the afternoon newspaper, *La Estrella.* What a surprise. Ty and I were on the cover smiling broadly. The caption described our dramatic voyage around Cape Horn in a tiny sailboat. "Not bad," Oz remarked. "Same-day celebrity status." The rest of the afternoon is somewhat blurry. We drank a staggering amount of good, cheap, local wine and feasted on delicious shellfish before I finally dragged Molly off to bed.

The telephone rang early the next morning and I decided to just let it ring. The caller was annoyingly persistent, and finally I answered it. "Hola, capitan," then rapid-fire Spanish came at me.

"Hold on, senor, no hablo Espanol."

"Oh, excuse me," came the reply in perfect English, "but I am a reporter from *La Estrella,* and we heard a rumor that you and your North American sweetheart plan to marry in Chile. Is that true?"

You've got to be kidding, I thought to myself. Then I said simply, "Yes, it is true."

"Oh, that's great. Can we have the exclusive story?"

"It's yours, my friend." I agreed to meet him at the boat the next day. Then I hung up the phone and pulled Molly close to me, just to be sure I wasn't dreaming.

Vina del Mar is a couple of miles north of Valparaiso. Both cities have close to 300,000 residents and border the Pacific, but those are the only similarities. Valparaiso is an historic port city, and for centuries commercial vessels have called at her inner harbor. Swift clippers, sturdy squareriggers of the late nineteenth century, and steamers have all etched their way into the city's history. The city has retained its European architecture and attitude. With patience, any fitting or spare part can eventually be found in Valparaiso.

Vina del Mar is Chile's playground for the rich. It is an exclusive resort town, with extravagant shops, expensive restaurants, and trendy people strutting about. Vina del Mar is an exciting town for wining and dining, but Valparaiso is by far the more interesting city.

Molly and I met with the reporter on the boat while Oz and Ty drove into Valparaiso in search of rubber gasket material, among other things. The reporter asked us vital questions such as why we wanted to marry in Chile, and what did I think of Chilean women?

I answered the latter question diplomatically, "Chilean women seem to be very beautiful and very charming, but not quite as beautiful as Molly." We posed for several embarrassing pictures, hugging and kissing, before the interview finally concluded.

"I'm glad that's over with," I said to Molly. "That was ridiculous. I bet it doesn't even make the paper." That afternoon, pictures of Molly and me were plastered all over *La Estrella.* Our wedding was their lead story. Obviously, the government-controlled paper was lacking in hard news that day.

Mom and Tim were scheduled to arrive in a couple of days, on

February 19, and we wanted to have all the wedding details ironed out before then. Molly had contacted the Chilean Consulate in New York before she left the States, and had been assured that the only legal requirement for us to marry in Chile was that we both obtain an international health certificate. Molly took a physical examination in the States, and I received the doctor's blessing in Vina del Mar. Our plan was to have a simple civil ceremony and a party afterward.

With certificates in hand documenting our healthy way of life, we drove to the civil registrar's office in Vina del Mar to apply for a marriage certificate. Surprise! The clerk told us that we had to fulfill a 90-day residency requirement before we would be issued a license. Molly tried to explain, in her best Spanish, about our voyage, and how it was impossible for us to stay in Chile for 90 days. When the clerk shrugged her shoulders, I demanded to see her superior. The manager was very sympathetic, especially when we showed her the paper clippings, but said simply, "Laws are laws. There is nothing I can do. The man in New York gave you the wrong information. I am sorry."

"I know how to resolve this," I said as we left the office. "Let's go see the Port Captain. He'll be able to pull some strings."

Patrico Gonzales was quite taken with Molly and assured us that he would take care of everything. "No more problems," he said soothingly, as he winked at Molly. We posed for more pictures before the Port Captain had us driven to the registrar's office in Valparaiso in his private car. I was certain we would walk in and our marriage license would already be typed up, waiting for us.

Unfortunately, the Port Captain's influence was not as great as he let on. We ran into the same roadblock — 90 days residency or no license. The Chilean government and the Catholic Church want you to be very sure you are ready for marriage, because divorce is against the law! As we pleaded our case to one stone-faced bureaucrat after another, Molly pulled me aside and whispered in my ear, "Maybe you should offer a bribe."

"No," I said, indignant. "Damn, Mol, we are not going to bribe our way into marriage." We stomped out of the building and returned to the Hotel O'Higgins.

We joined Ty and Oz for lunch and explained our frustrating morning. "The only way to get things accomplished in a foreign country is to go through the American Consulate," Ty assured us. He suggested we drive to Santiago, the capital, and explain our unique situation to someone in the consulate. I took him up on his offer of assistance, figuring if Ty couldn't find a way around the law, nobody could.

The following morning we set off for Santiago. We were obliged to present our passports at several police roadblocks, but our papers were in order and we were not hassled. Santiago is a bustling city of 4,000,000 people, and has the same vitality as other major South American urban centers. Street peddlers with push carts vie for space among the taxis and buses on the congested streets, which are choked with diesel fumes. The military government makes its presence known with many armed soldiers quietly patrolling the city. It took us a couple of hours to locate the consulate. We met with the liaison officer for Americans in Chile. She, too, was most sympathetic with our plight, but not very optimistic. She arranged a meeting for us with the consulate general, Mr. Don Bean. Also, as a last resort, she gave Molly the telephone number of a priest who was known to have greasy palms.

The security at the consulate was alarming. We had to leave all of our possessions at the guardhouse, and then go through two friskings before we were allowed to enter. We had the audacity to arrive 15 minutes early for our appointment, and for some reason this really irked Mr. Bean. At 2:00 P.M. on the minute, he showed us into his office, saying, "I don't like you standing around out there; you're early, you know." We apologized.

I explained the situation, but Mr. Bean misunderstood, and thought we were trying to get divorced.

"It's a crazy world today; all you young people trying to get out of marriage, not into it. It's against the law in this country to divorce, which is idiotic, but, well, it's the law."

I finally made him understand that we wanted to get married. "Oh, well, that's a horse of a different color. There's a dilemma for you, that crazy residency law. Don't know if I can help you much on that one. I'll tell you what, I'll beat around the bushes and get back to you. Where did you say you were staying? Valpo?

"Now, let me tell you about the food here." Politely, we then endured a 20-minute oration about what to, and what not to eat in Chile, before we wrangled free of Mr. Don Bean. It was easier to understand the sorry state of our international relations after meeting with this high-ranking diplomat.

Back at the O'Higgins, Mom and Tim had arrived. It was great to wrap my arms around my mother. I had not seen her in almost a year. She and Tim had as many sea stories as we did. After they completed the refit of the *Epoch* in Ft. Lauderdale, they set sail in June, bound around the world. They sailed through the Yucatan Channel to Cozumel, and then on to Panama. They transited the Canal, the *Epoch*'s third run

Right to left: Jeanne Kretschmer, Molly, John, Ty, and Oz take time out for lunch in Vina del Mar.

through the isthmus, and then went offshore in the Pacific to the Galapagos. They continued westward to the Marquesas, completing a 3,000-mile passage. Then they threaded their way through the dangerous Tuamotu Archipelago before reaching the Society Islands. *Epoch* was currently moored in Tahiti.

Mom looked 20 years younger and Tim seemed to defy the aging process. For a couply of sixty-year-olds, they have more energy and spunk than most of us. I was thrilled to see the sparkle in Mom's eyes. For the first time since the death of my father nine years before, she wasn't lonely.

Molly explained our somewhat comical pursuit of a marriage license. "It's kind of ironic," Mom commented, "that you kids, who have always lived just outside society's boundaries, should be thwarted in your one stab at conformity." I told Mom I had one last idea. I remembered that merchant sea captains had the legal right to perform marriages, and Molly and I drove down to the wharf in Valparaiso in search of a romantic captain.

We sneaked past the guardhouse and wandered about the crates and

Oz at work aboard Gigi.

cranes along the wharf. Molly spotted a white and red freighter flying the American flag. The chief engineer welcomed us aboard and introduced us to the captain.

"I know this will sound somewhat unusual," I said with a smile, "but would you be willing to marry us?" Then I explained our voyage and our frustrating attempts to secure a marriage license.

"Sorry, skipper," the captain replied, "but captains only perform weddings in the movies today; insurance companies just won't let us touch that kind of stuff anymore."

Driving back to the O'Higgins, we were both discouraged and completely out of bright ideas. For the most part we were silent.

When I drove right past the O'Higgins, Molly asked, "Where are you headed, baby?"

"I don't know. Let's just take a ride." We drove north of the quaint fishing village of Con Con, until we came upon a vast expanse of wide open beach. I parked the car and we walked hand in hand down to the sea. The surf was magnificent as powerful breakers crashed ashore. The beach was more than a quarter mile wide and completely undeveloped.

"This would be a lovely spot to get married," Molly said softly, and snuggled next to me.

"Yes, it sure is, baby. Hey, Mol?"

"Yes?"

"Let's just marry ourselves. We don't need a silly, official document from the civil registrar. I love you, Molly, and I always will and I just want you to know that."

"Johnny, that sounds wonderful. Oh, baby, I love you, too. I'll love you until the sun's gone. Let's marry ourselves right here on this beach."

Molly took my hand and started running back to the car. "Come on, we'll tell everyone we're getting married tomorrow."

Later that afternoon, Molly and Mom went off in pursuit of a wedding dress, and Oz and I drove Ty to the airport in Santiago. Unfortunately, Ty had to leave that night or else remain at least another week in Chile. A mechanics' strike had grounded most of the flights out of the country. We dropped him off at the terminal and I helped him with his luggage. An impatient driver behind us was rudely honking his horn, so we had to cut our farewells short.

"Thanks for everything, Ty. I'll get *Gigi* to San Francisco for you. You can count on that."

"I know you will, John. That was a wild ride we had together. I'll never forget it. Take care. Goodbye."

Mom, Tim, Oz, Molly, and I all crowded into the rent-a-car the early afternoon of February 23, 1984. We drove to the Playa Ritoque, our special beach. However, as we hiked out to the spot Molly and I had picked out the day before, we were horrified to find the Chilean Marines practicing assault landings on the beach. Before we could nonchalantly turn around and scurry down the beach, a soldier, waving his rifle over his head, came charging toward us. He noticed Oz's camera dangling from his neck, and hollered at him, "No fotos, no fotos!"

"OK, partner, no sweat. No pictures," Oz said calmly, trying to placate the excited marine, who insisted on removing the film from the camera and emphatically gestured for us to move up the beach.

"Christ," Oz mumbled, as we hiked away from the marines. A mile up the beach we found a perfect location for the ceremony.

We were hidden from the marines by a small dune, but we still had a clear view of the crashing surf and the vast Pacific. It was crystal clear,

A wedding on a beach, and the crew of the Epoch *reunited.*

and the ocean and sky were the same shade of deep blue. Mom and Tim set up a picnic lunch, while Oz reloaded his camera. Molly and I stood side by side on a small knoll, our backs to the sea.

While I appeared slightly awkward in my fancy shirt and trousers, Molly looked positively beautiful in her sheer, white, embroidered peasant dress. The ceremony was entirely freelance. After a bit of silence, I spoke up.

"Molly, I wrote this song when I was south of Cape Horn. I think the Horn was easy on us because it knew how much I wanted to get back to you. Well, here goes. It's called 'Molly's Song':

"I am a wandering albatross, destined to soar over the deep blue sea,
I plot my course by the sun and stars, but only my lover can set me free.
I'm sailing alone on this winged flight, spiraling skyward to stars above,
Throughout the storms, you're my guiding light, you are my Molly, my only true love.

The sky is gray and the sea is steel blue, off to starboard, I see storm-tossed Cape Horn,
We're hard on the wind, just trying to make way, and I'm thinking of you on this cold, blustery morn.
You are a wandering albatross, sailing alone on your winged flight,
You roam the ocean and you roam the shore, let's sail together off into the night.

We'll follow a flyway that's uniquely ours, some may condemn us, but what do they know?
We have no anchors, and we're searching for the stars, alone together, our love will just grow.
I am a wandering albatross, you're a wandering albatross,
We're destined to soar over the deep blue sea,
We'll sail together and we'll sail free,
We'll sail together and we'll sail forever."

Then it was Molly's turn. Nervously, she shifted her feet in the sand. She smiled and pulled at her sleeve. She spoke softly at first, but as she spoke her voice sang out to me.

"I watch the ocean's fury unfurl at the shore, and coalesce with magic as it bursts against a granite wedge. And on another day, it lulls us with tranquility and makes a promise of friendship until darkness, when its mood becomes volatile and restless with energy.

She sleeps in the sun and glitters like a child's eyes, and cradles foreign continents with shoulders of liquid steel. And when we cast off our moorings and the burdens of terrestrial existence, you and I will know, that somewhere there's a chalice hidden in the sand, somewhere there's mystery we cannot understand. There are answers to our questions, and riddles left to solve, and budding ambitions beginning to evolve. We shall make discoveries, we shall comb the seas, the world is our playground, and our vehicle is the breeze.

Take the sun and cast it on the water. In a boat, like a stone, we shall skip across the bluest horizons."

We were married. Maybe we didn't have the blessing of the state, but we had each other, forever.

10

Becalmed

MOLLY AND I DISAPPEARED. We checked into a hotel just down the street from the O'Higgins, but nobody, and I mean nobody, was permitted to cross our threshold. We spent three blissful days in solitude, loving, lounging, and dreaming. For the first time in six months, I thought of things other than winds, currents, and courses. Molly massaged my aching muscles, and we talked and talked, remembering the old days and planning the days to come. It was easy to overlook the final leg of our voyage, for there was no disputing it, the 6,000-mile homestretch looked decidedly anticlimatic. How could we have known that the third leg of our long journey would prove to be the most challenging of all?

After our all-too-brief honeymoon, we joined Mom and Tim for a jaunt into the Andes. Oz remained in Vina del Mar to continue working on *Gigi* and to try to recover from a miserable stomach virus that never let him stray far from the head. Our well-used Toyota rent-a-car lumbered over the coastal mountain range and onto the central plateau. Once west of Santiago, the countryside was quite rural. Our destination was Portillo, a famous ski resort nestled on a ridge halfway up Mt. Aconcagua, South America's highest peak, straddling the Argentina-

Chile border. We followed a tortuous, switchbacking road up to Portillo. It was late summer in the Andes, and the rustic lodge was nearly deserted. We rented a cozy chalet overlooking a deep blue glacial lake.

Twelve thousand feet above sea level I had to quell a desperate urge to return to the ocean. My world was a watery one, and I felt strangely out of place in the mountains. Standing on the veranda of our cottage, I watched the sun's shadow recede down the barren face of a rocky canyon. Like the setting sun, our voyage was entering the final act. I was ready to play my part, and it was time to raise the curtain.

We returned to Santiago on February 27, after just a couple days in Portillo, and dropped Mom and Tim at the airport. They had their own voyage to pursue, and I could tell Tim was worried about the *Epoch.* I shook his hand and then hugged my mother. "Thanks so much for coming, Ma, it really meant a lot to me."

"Oh, Johnny, I wouldn't have missed this for the world. You two are my special kids. Now remember, my son, this is the last leg; sail cautiously. I am very proud of you, Johnny. Goodbye."

Watching Mom and Tim board the plane, Molly remarked, "It's amazing — you and your mom are cut from the same mold."

"Ya, and they should probably break the mold now before any more damage is done." Seriously, Molly's observation was very accurate. Mom and I are an enigma to the rest of the family. My brothers and sisters are always loving and supportive, but I don't think they understand our unquenchable desire to reach beyond the distant horizon. I'm not sure I understand it either. Wanderlust is something you must be cursed with from birth.

Oz had *Gigi* in shipshape condition when we returned, and we spent all day February 28 provisioning. The supermarket in Vina del Mar was clean, modern, and well stocked. For fresh produce, we drove into Valparaiso and visited the sprawling, open air mercado. Agriculturally, Chile is fertile and productive, and the mercado was bustling. The vast array of fruits and vegetables was most impressive. We stocked up on apples, oranges, grapefruit, lemons, and limes, as well as potatoes, carrots, beans, and onions.

Molly assumed responsibility for stowing everything aboard. After stashing the canned and packaged goods beneath the settees, she washed every piece of fruit and vegetable in a diluted bleach mix, and then carefully wrapped it in newspaper. She stowed the produce in hammocks in the saloon, taking care to place the most perishable items on top.

Obtaining fresh water proved to be a problem. The water at the club wasn't potable, and the city water truck insisted on delivering a minimum of 500 gallons, which was about 450 gallons more than we needed. We ended up purchasing bottled water, specifically 12 cases or 144, 1.5-liter bottles, for a total of about 57 gallons. Storing the bottles below required the utmost creativity. Much to Molly's and Oz's chagrin, I decided to leave most of the water in bottles, instead of emptying it into the tanks. It would be easy to monitor our consumption and impossible to foul. However, when I passed the last bottle below, I wondered where Oz and I were going to live for the next six or seven weeks.

Just before sunset, *Gigi* settled deep into the water. With all of our provisions and supplies aboard, she looked like she had just eaten at a churrascaria. Our plan was to hit the watery trail in the morning, but our plans were literally jolted when we were unexpectedly struck by lightning. The bolt that nailed us was 19 feet long, fiberglass, and helmed by a neophyte. The yacht club's fleet Lightnings had just completed a regatta and were recklessly tacking up the narrow channel to the clubhouse. Chilean sailors have a curious concept of right of way, and seem to prefer smashing into each other instead of falling off the mark. Unfortunately, Lightning #1126 held her course a bit too long, and before she could come about she collided with *Gigi* and dealt a jarring blow to the steering vane mounted on the stern. Angrily, I fended off, but my heart sank because I knew it was a moment too late. I hastily pulled the vane paddle from the water and examined it. I wanted to scream; the stainless steel strap that controls the trim rudder was crushed!

In the meantime, the three embarrassed sailors in the Lightning had drifted into irons. I scowled at them, but they avoided meeting my eyes. But what could I do? The club's hospitality had been marvelous, and obviously, if anyone was to blame it was me. I should have had the rudder stowed on deck. My frown fell away, and I waved at the three youngsters and gestured that everything was all right. The sorry truth: Without the trim tab control, the steering vane would never hold a course.

"John," Molly said softly, "you'll never find a replacement part in Chile."

"I know, baby, but it's not just the strap. I think we might be able to improvise, but even if we can, we'll have to weld it back in place, and stainless to stainless welding can be very tricky."

"Ahoy, amigos," came the call from the dock. A short, plump, well-dressed man with a captain's cap set jauntily on his head, waved at us. "I saw that unfortunate incident a few minutes ago. I sure hope there wasn't any damage to your boat. I know all about your expedition from the newspaper accounts. May I come aboard?"

"Welcome aboard," I said with a distinct lack of enthusiasm. "Oh boy, all we need is some local yokel to try and tell us what to do," I thought to myself.

"My name is Mario. That's my 30-foot sloop over there," he said, pointing at a weathered old C & C. "I can't believe how small your boat is," he commented. "No offense, but even I can just barely stand up." I gave Mario a brief tour of *Gigi* (pun intended), and then showed him the damaged vane paddle. He examined it carefully and confidently blurted out, "No problem here, my friends. We need a piece of stainless steel. It's just 316 grade stainless, and we need a good welder, too. Come along, I know where we can find both."

"But it's already past 6:00," I protested.

Mario just waved his hand, slung the vane paddle over his shoulder, and quickly waddled down the dock. I grabbed my wallet and hurried after him. As we drove into Valparaiso, Mario explained that he was born in Chile, but had lived most of his adult life in New York and Los Angeles. He was a naturalized American citizen, very patriotic and a fierce Dodgers fan. He was in Chile on a two-year assignment for Birdseye Foods.

"Chile is a sleeping giant. One day she'll be the breadbasket, or at least the fruitbasket, of the world!"

Mario wound his way up and down the narrow alleys of the industrial district. He finally screeched to a halt in front of a run-down machine shop. The lone employee, or maybe he was the proprietor, sat slouched over, fast asleep on the step.

"Wake up, amigo," Mario howled cheerfully.

The old man came to his senses as Mario explained the problem. We followed him into the dirty shop, and he picked up a piece of dusty steel off the floor. Mario examined it and gave the thumbs-up sign. The old man hastily made a few measurements, and then cut the stainless steel to match the trim tab strap. Then he promptly fired up his ancient arc welder and welded the new strap to the vane. It didn't look pretty, but it sure looked strong.

"He says there is no charge," Mario told me. "He says you are a braver man than he is, and he just wants to shake your hand."

Mario dropped me off at the yacht club, and I thanked him sincerely for his help. "Just do one thing for me," he asked. "Please drop me a note when you reach San Francisco."

We were up with the sun on February 29, the day of the leap year. After breakfast, we cleared customs and returned the rent-a-car. Then it was time to say goodbye to Molly, again. She was scheduled to take a bus into Santiago and then catch a flight to Texas. She was going to live aboard Oz's 42-foot ketch on Galveston Bay. She had promised to do the brightwork if Oz gave her unlimited use of his Corvette. Surprisingly, neither one of us was melancholy. I took her into my arms and kissed her. Just knowing that this would be the last time we would have to say goodbye eased the pain.

Molly cast off the bow lines, and *Gigi* sluggishly made her way for the open sea. We were loaded to the gunwales, and 6,000 miles of vast Pacific Ocean lay ahead of us. Before sunset the coast of Chile was only a memory — *Gigi* was back in her element. On the first watch I seriously considered the long passage ahead. I envisioned an ideal tradewind romp to the equator, and once through the doldrums, a swift beat north to San Francisco. I anticipated a 45- to 50-day passage. Ah, but what an optimist I was. Once again I had underestimated the resolve of Neptune. If I had known that it would take 10½ maddening weeks to reach the Golden Gate, I would have stayed in the Andes.

Oz and I are both sturdy 200-pounders, and readjusting to life at sea aboard cramped *Gigi* was tough. Down below we had our choice of three positions: we could lie down, sit at the chart table, or stand crouched in the galley — that was it. Luckily, we picked up fresh offshore breezes, and rattled off 400 miles the first three days out. The lack of creature comforts are much more tolerable when you're reaching along at hull speed.

Unfortunately, we suffered a crucial blow on March 2. Our workhorse spinnaker, a multicolored, tri-radial, 1½-ounce chute, fell victim to a sudden 25-knot gust. We had just one other spinnaker aboard, a broad-shouldered, lightweight chute, and I never expected it to endure the steady tradewinds. Despite this potential handicap, Oz and I began to dream up outrageous ETAs. Maybe, just maybe, we'd average 140 miles a day, and fetch San Francisco in less than 40 days? I think our boastful projections offended the ocean, because on March 3, the wind and seas went flat.

We charted a course, carefully following the advice of *Ocean Passages for the World*. We shaped a northwesterly track out of Valparaiso to take advantage of the strong Peruvian Current. Specifically, *Ocean Passages* recommends crossing the 20th parallel south at 85° west. I sketched this route onto a small-scale plotting chart, and dutifully we steered *Gigi* along the thin graphite line. Unfortunately, the winds didn't always agree with the British Hydrographic Department.

The noon fix on March 5 put us 45 miles northeast of San Ambrosia, a small offshore island. The wind was light from the southeast, and as *Gigi* plodded along, I came to understand why clipper ship captains dreaded making landfall along the west coast of South America. By closing the coast, captains knew they might spend weeks recapturing "westing" lost by not sailing directly northwest from Cape Horn. Amazingly, Valparaiso is actually east of New York. We needed to traverse not only 70° of latitude, but also 52° of longitude before we reached San Francisco.

Despite the light conditions, I was at first reluctant to fly our remaining spinnaker. I couldn't bear the thought of blowing out both chutes on the first week of the passage. Contrary to many offshore sailors, I am a firm believer in spinnakers. A well-trimmed chute can spell the difference between an extremely frustrating 75-mile run and a gratifying 120-mile run. Many cruising references speak of spinnakers as though they are sinister sails, necessitating 10 burly crewmembers to handle them. Instead, they recommend the awkward, twin headsail rig for downwind sailing. This is sheer nonsense. The only difficult aspect of handling a chute is the pole, so why would anyone want to deal with two of them? A properly rigged chute can be an exhilarating offshore experience. Of course, it's vital to watch the weather and douse the chute before things turn nasty. Today's spinnaker scoopers and poleless cruising chutes make spinnaker sailing easier than ever.

On March 6, Oz spotted a fishing boat to port. Little did we know that it would be the last vessel we would set eyes on for more than 40 days. The wind remained annoyingly light, and we capped our first week at sea with a dismal run of just 65 miles. After that, we flew our spinnaker at every opportunity, but our daily average had already dropped to 108 miles. (Because of the length of the passage, we hoarded our diesel fuel for charging the batteries.) So much for our 140-mile-a-day predictions.

Patiently, and sometimes not so patiently, we searched for the tradewinds. With every emerging zephyr we would write hopefully in the log: "Looks like we have finally found the trades," or, "Maybe the trades?" and finally, "Please be the trades!" According to both *Ocean Passages* and the pilot chart, we should have been well within the southern limit of the southeast tradewinds, but there just wasn't any wind. To ward off the blues I staged an imaginary race with the sun. Our objective was to beat the sun to the equator before the March 22 vernal equinox. However, on March 8 and 9 we managed just 77 and 74 miles respectively, and the sun left us in its shadow and never looked back.

On March 9 we commenced the first of many assaults on the tenacious barnacles clinging to *Gigi*'s bottom. What began as an afternoon swim on a calm day, turned into a nightmare, as we discovered thick slime and marine growth below the waterline. While one of us would dive below and furiously attack the barnacles with a makeshift scraper, the other would tread water and look for sharks!

The sorry state of the bottom was a keen disappointment and a constant aggravation as we tried to coax *Gigi* along in light airs. We chipped off a lot of paint by scraping, thus exposing the unprotected hull to the persistent ravishes of barnacles. I chastised myself for not hauling the boat at the yacht club, but I never imagined the paint would fail so miserably. Nine months before, in Detroit, we had had the bottom professionally painted, and when I dove over the side in the South Atlantic only a month ago, the hull had been as smooth as a baby's bottom. However, as *Gigi* drifted north, she was more akin to a floating botanical garden than a finely tuned offshore racing yacht.

(In San Francisco, the manufacturer of the paint supplied us with a shaky explanation of why their product had failed. The waters off Chile have an overabundance of copper in them because the country is the world's largest copper producer. The paint people feel that somehow the copper in the water reacted chemically with the copper-based paint, and completely shut down the antifouling system!)

Many people ask me, "What do you do all day long out there on the ocean?" The answer is simple — work! For example, I spent the morning of March 10 repairing a crack in the fiberglass vane paddle, and the rest of the day stitching up our 1½-ounce spinnaker. It was a massive repair job, and well beyond the realm of my less than amateur sail-repair skills, but I tackled it anyway. Oz and I had a brief spat when I asked him to help and he refused. He claimed he didn't know how to sew. I finally finished my handiwork just before dinner. I was feeling somewhat smug; the repair looked pretty good. I hauled the sail onto the foredeck and attached the sheets, guys, and halyard. Then I hoisted it into the air. It was beautiful. The patched-up spinnaker caught the wind and started to pull *Gigi* forward like huskies before a sled. Then suddenly — Boom! It exploded like a shotgun. The sail was shredded. Dejectedly, I gathered up the ragged pieces of nylon, stuffed them into the turtle and shoved the whole mess into the forepeak.

The next night I thought my worst fears had come true. *Gigi* was reaching along silently, propelled by her sprawling, bright red, Stroh's-decorated spinnaker. Oz had just assumed watch duty, and I was almost asleep when I heard a loud bang!

"Oh, no," I thought, "there goes the other chute." I dashed on deck, but Oz was already forward scooping the sail out of the water. We were relieved to find that the spinnaker was intact; the shackle on the halyard had parted and dropped the chute into the drink.

After his watch, Oz wrote in the log: "Thank God, the Stroh's bear is still with us." I read his entry and chuckled. The Stroh's bear he mentioned was supposed to be our sponsor's trademark, a lion. The gold, larger-than-life lion stitched to the belly of the spinnaker was an odd looking fellow, not resembling the lion on the beer cans. The more I thought about it, Oz was right, it did look like a bear. We started to call the spinnaker the "dancing bear."

In the morning Oz hoisted me up to the masthead, and I retrieved the errant halyard. Clutching the spar in rolling seas, I couldn't help but think of the unfortunate sailors who shipped out before the mast on the towering clipper ships. They spent a lot of time aloft, not just 40 feet above the deck, but sometimes as high as 200 feet! Perched on narrow footropes, with many men to a yard, they battled stiff canvas sails in all weather conditions. When I was safely back on deck, I resolved to secure the halyard to the head of the chute with a stout bowline and avoid another trip up the mast.

On March 12, I placed a call on the SSB to my brother Ed in Ann Arbor, Michigan. I had a premonition that I should call home, and sure enough, Eddy was the bearer of sad news. My grandfather had died the day before. Gramps, my mom's dad, was my very special friend. He was a free-spirited old man, and fiercely independent. He was also an enthusiastic supporter of my wayward lifestyle. I loved him dearly. The Pacific Ocean is vast all right, but it is also ever so confining. That night it was a giant prison cell. I spent my watch sitting on the forward hatch, remembering Gramps and crying. I wanted to be anywhere but aboard *Gigi* just then.

Grampa's death seemed particularly unfair to me, although all death seems unfair. Still, my grandfather would never know the notoriety our voyage received. He would not see our pictures in the newspaper and listen to us on radio and television shows. To be sure, the little vanities of recognition are not very significant, but to a sick old man, gently rocking in a nursing home, it would have meant a lot. I am no stranger to death. My father died when I was sixteen, and my sister died five years later after a bitter struggle with breast cancer. Watching them die had reminded me of my own mortality, and maybe that is why I've chosen to live my life out of the mainstream.

On March 18, *Gigi* finally found the long-awaited southeast tradewinds. We followed the dancing bear, and despite her foul bottom, *Gigi* rolled along downwind at 5 and 6 knots. Even though the trades were two weeks overdue, I knew I was feeling better when I started to sing on watch again. Another reason we endured the unexpected two weeks of light air was because Oz took his role as cook very seriously. He creatively churned out one delicious meal after another. He baked fresh bread at least twice a week, but Sunday brunch was his specialty. Every Sunday he would wake up early and start baking. Then he'd rustle up whopping portions of eggs, canned bacon, packaged hashbrowns, and even pancakes. Oh yes, he also served a stiff pitcher of Bloody Marys to wash it all down with. Oz kept up these weekly feasts throughout the voyage, until we ran dangerously low on foodstuffs.

Nothing shakes the blues from a sailor faster than 20 knots over the transom. When the wind gusted above 20 knots, we doused the dancing bear and poled out the genoa in its place. Flying fish on the deck are a sure sign of tradewind sailing, and one morning I scooped 16 fish off the deck. A few were still alive and hesitantly swam away when I pitched them overboard. What a surprise it must have been to finally elude a predator by breaking the surface of the water and, just as they felt the freedom of flight, to smash into *Gigi*'s hull! I wondered what the odds were of both of us being in the same place at the same time? Probably about the same as *Gigi* getting run down by a freighter; then I decided not to think about it any more.

March 22, 23, and 24 were the best sailing days of the passage as we logged 412 miles. However, on March 25, the day we passed the halfway point to San Francisco, the weather turned squally and the wind shifted to the west. I had a disturbing hunch that our tradewind ride was about to be abruptly cut short. Unfortunately, I was right.

For 48 hours we endured constant rain as the wind slowly diminished. We replenished our water supply and took glorious freshwater showers, but I was horrified to be encountering doldrumlike conditions 250 miles south of the equator. On March 28 we awoke to find a placid sea; *Gigi* was firmly entrenched in the dreary equatorial doldrums. Our tradewind ride had lasted a paltry eight days. The prospect of a long, slow haul through the doldrums seemed inevitable.

We had precious little diesel fuel, and we restricted motoring to brief spurts just to break the monotony of bobbing becalmed. We also refrained from using the SSB, which required a lot of power. I began to crave a conversation with Molly. I needed to hear her voice. The equator is just not the place to be if you're in a hurry, and I was in a hurry. Oz and I passed the time by playing Yahtzee, and still dreamed about a 50-day passage.

One month out of Valparaiso, we polished off the last of the fresh fruit. Our snail-like progress was exasperating. Many clipper ship captains were driven to near madness as their ships lay stranded in the doldrums. I sympathized with them. I vented my frustration in the form of anger. At night I would shout obscenities at the sea and plead for wind. On March 30, we managed just 64 miles; the next day we drifted just 22 miles farther; and on April 1, we made just 18 miles more.

For three days in a row I thought we had crossed the equator, only to find out at noon that we were still in the southern hemisphere. We were battling a mysterious current that wreaked havoc with my dead reckoning. I abandoned my sextant in favor of a funnel. When the water flowed clockwise down the funnel, I knew we had finally crossed the line. Unfortunately, we wasted an entire bottle of Scotch celebrating the false crossings.

A list of our daily runs describes the frustration of the doldrums more accurately than adjectives:

```
March  27 — 73  miles
       28 — 79
       29 — 97
       30 — 64
       31 — 22
April   1 — 18
        2 — 60
        3 — 45
        4 — 78
        5 — 46
        6 —  6
        7 — 75
        8 — 54
        9 — 74
```

In one seven-day period we totaled just 275 miles. That breaks down to 39 miles a day, or 1.6 knots an hour for a week! On April 6, our noon to noon run was 6 miles. The garbage we threw overboard at dinner was still in view in the morning.

You often hear sailors spin yarns about terrible, survival storms, but given the choice between calms and storms, I'd choose the latter. When the weather is rough, every moment aboard is filled with vitality. Immediate decisions have immediate consequences. During the height of a gale, you can feel how fragile your grip on existence really is. By contrast, days and weeks of calms are almost intolerable. Inactivity and boredom turn to apathy as one day melts unnoticeably into the next. After a while, you don't even bother to hoist the sails; the annoying slatting of Dacron only serves to remind you of your misery. Stranded on a

Gigi *bobs becalmed in the Pacific.*

small boat on a placid ocean, you begin to question your motives for making such a voyage.

The emotional strain of the slow passage eventually caught up with us. Oz and I had trouble communicating right from the start. He is an intensely private man and wastes few words; he has a tendency to get right to the point when he speaks. Therefore, when he mentioned *Gigi* seemed worn out, I knew he meant it. I exploded, "Worn out? Christ, Oz, this boat is less than 16 months old, and she has already logged 20,000 miles. She's beat down the English Channel against the November gales, and she's rounded the Horn to windward. Right now I wouldn't hesitate to sail her anywhere."

"Take it easy, John," Oz replied. "I didn't say she wasn't a damn fine little boat, but she does need some work. You don't have to take it personally."

But I did take it personally. Although *Gigi* was Ty's boat on paper, I felt that only I knew her inside and out. We'd been through so much together that I just couldn't tolerate anyone's lack of respect for her.

Oz and I quibbled over other things. He questioned my navigational tactics and thought we should head east and hug the coast. I knew very well from experience that the western coast of Central America is one of the calmest on earth. What we really needed was more westing, but when the winds blew at all, they came primarily from the west. Another problem we had was a generation gap. Oz is fifty years old and he has a son my age. He's been very successful in business and with private investments; indeed, you might say he has a Midas touch. It was difficult for him to take orders from a captain half his age. Still, I never shy away from responsibility on a boat, and one thing I've learned is that the captain must be captain.

Although calm weather reveals many of the ocean's creatures that otherwise go unnoticed, even dolphins, manta rays, whales and sea birds couldn't lift our spirits. The truth is, wind is the cure-all for all that ails disgruntled sailors. We crossed the 10th parallel at 118° west and finally picked up stronger winds. Even though the northerlies were direct head winds, it was a great relief to feel *Gigi* heel hard to port and charge forward. Shipboard activities resumed their urgencies, and our nagging, petty differences vanished with the calms.

Oz tapped my shoulder for the midnight watch on April 12. He stood at the chart table as I slipped on my safety harness.

"I made you a spot of tea, Captain."

"Thanks, Oz."

"Don't mention it. You know, I was just thinking, it's a good thing it's not 1849. If we were heading to San Francisco to stake a claim, all the gold would be gone before we got there."

On Friday, April 13, we found ourselves laughing at the sly humor of cartographers. According to my sights, we were about 20 miles west of an obscure, isolated rock with the grand name of "Ville de Toulouse," and followed by "ED." Although we were more than 1,000 miles offshore, we scanned the horizon for any signs of land. I looked up the initials "ED" in *Bowditch,* and learned that they stand for "existence doubtful."

"Ville de Toulouse" was probably just a mirage to a very weary French navigator.

On my watch that night, I wrote a letter to Molly by the light of the full moon. The moon must have been affecting me more than I knew, because I told Molly that I wished she was on Ville de Toulouse waiting for me. My prose eventually turned into a rambling verse:

"Moods and states of mind and winds and changing tides. Is it GMT or LMT? Are we pinching up or can we run free? I write you letters

and write the log, noting the weather and such. But has my blind am-
bition obscured the ocean's subtle touch? I've cursed and screamed
at the fickle sea, pleading for winds to suit me. It's too easy to let the
hours pass, kind of like skipping class.

Still, I'm proud to have sailed this many a mile. God, if he's about,
probably laughs at my style.

I'm searching for you in the face of every wave, my distant lover. Are
you on Ville de Toulouse? No. I fear you've gone undercover. There
is still a watery chasm of 1,500 miles that separates us. Oh, but mind
you, my lover, I'll bridge that gap, I must. I am coming, Gigi *is com-*
ing. Yes we're coming, Gigi *and me and the gulls and the seaweed.*
We're all coming, baby, we're all coming."

On April 15, we spotted a freighter, the *Iceland.* Ironically, we
hadn't seen a ship in 40 days, but if we had not fallen off the wind we
would have been on a collision course. I hailed the captain on the VHF
radio, and he seemed shocked that we were so far offshore. I was
disgusted with his lack of knowledge of global wind patterns. Few merchant seamen today understand the sea and her many moods as well as
their ancestors, the hard-driving sailors who plied the ocean under sail.

Later that afternoon, we took an inventory of our remaining food
supplies. Obviously, our slow progress had depleted our reserves, but a
careful examination revealed how critical the situation had become. We
were completely out of fresh foods, and our supply of canned meats and
vegetables would only last us 20 days, at most. We were 45 days en route,
and we still had 1,500 miles to go. We decided to ration ourselves to one
meal a day, a meal that grew more meager every day our trip dragged on.

From the time *Gigi* had entered the doldrums three weeks before,
we'd encountered head winds every day as we worked northward. The
weather patterns just didn't make sense. A possible explanation for the
unpredictable winds we had encountered might lie in the lingering effect
of "El Nino." El Nino is a cyclical weather disturbance that occurs approximately every four or five years, and El Nino of 1982 and 1983 was
considered the worst ever. The entire world experienced dramatic
changes in weather, and no region was harder hit than the Pacific basin.
Meteorologists are not sure exactly what triggers an El Nino, but many
normal weather patterns in the Pacific were disturbed. The usually
strong and cold Peruvian Current lost much of its zip and turned warm.
The result was that many exotic species of wildlife in the Galapagos
Islands suffered grave casualties. The normal high-pressure tradewind
zone of the western Pacific failed to materialize, and the low pressure of
the eastern Pacific moved westward. As a result, Tahiti and her
neighboring islands were battered by six hurricanes, their first such

storms in 75 years. It was reasonable to assume that El Nino was at least partially to blame for our poor performance on Leg III.

On April 18, the wind gradually strengthened all day, and before midnight we had a full gale right on the nose. *Gigi* had trouble tracking to weather with her bottom so foul, and we constantly searched for that curious balance between course and speed. She seemed to sail best about 45 degrees off the apparent wind.

Propelled by the strong winds, we managed to sail more than 100 miles a day on both April 19 and 20. It was the first time we'd managed 100 miles in 23 days. On April 21, we required only three digits to tally up the mileage to San Francisco. Our celebration was short-lived because at dinner time Oz announced that our old nemesis, the totally unreliable kerosene stove, had done it again; it was clogged up. We consoled ourselves with the fact that we had very little food left to cook anyway. April 28 marked the end of our eighth week at sea and the beginning of our 28th straight day of beating!

Statistically, the passage had become a disaster. Our daily average had plunged to 86 miles. Our goal was simply to finish. We no longer counted the days or cared about records. On April 30, a hard northwest wind forced us to make a difficult decision. Our position was approximately 30° N, 128° W, or about 600 miles southwest of San Francisco. My instinct was to tack offshore, even though it meant heading due west and would add a lot of miles to our course. However, all signs pointed to a developing gale, and due to our lack of food supplies, we just couldn't risk getting caught well offshore. Reluctantly, we brought *Gigi* through the wind, and hardened the sheets. The best heading we could make was 040°, which pointed the bow at Point Conception.

That night a Force 8 gale came whistling down out of the north-northwest. Oz and I argued about how much sail we should carry. I was determined to make the most of the gale and drive *Gigi* to her limit. I knew quite well just how much sail she could carry, and with her foul bottom a single reef in the main and about 80 percent of the genoa kept us moving. Oz thought I was being reckless and he let me know about it. He wanted to reef way down, but I vetoed the idea. However, as soon as I went below after my watch he went forward and reduced the main down to the third row of reef points. I was furious, but I forced myself to stay in my bunk. It was an unlucky night for Oz because shortly after he finished reefing, the wind moderated a bit. Dutifully he went forward to shake out the reefs. He failed to untie all the reef points, however, and as he hoisted the mainsail, I heard a loud ripping sound. That was it; I jumped up and dashed into the cockpit.

"Goddamnit, Oz, why in the hell did you reef down in the first place?"

"I don't have to explain everything I do to you," Oz snapped back at me. In the meantime the sail was flogging in the wind.

"Are you just going to let the sail flog itself to death? Come on, Oz, you made a stupid mistake, now get your act together."

"Me get my act together? Mistake, ya, the only mistake I made was shipping on with you. You're a fucking tyrant."

I slammed the hatch and went below.

We changed watch later that night like silent sentries. Not a word was spoken. The tension between us was close to the breaking point, and we were both poised for a fight, a fist fight. In the morning we had another nasty exchange.

"I'll tell you something, John Kretschmer, you've got a helluva lot to learn about handling people, a helluva lot."

"Oh ya, and I suppose you're going to teach me?" I asked, insultingly.

"No, I'm not going to waste my time. Nobody can teach you a damn thing; you think you know everything already. Well, I'll tell you something — you don't."

April 30 was surely the longest day of the voyage — the hours wore on — an impenetrable silence accentuated our bitterness. It was crazy. Both of us had had our egos bruised, but we didn't hate each other; we'd just been at sea for too long. The next morning Oz let me oversleep, and somehow he managed to concoct an enormous breakfast, in the Sunday brunch tradition. It was our first good meal in more than a week.

"Breakfast time," Oz announced. I stumbled out of bed and pulled on a sweater. Oz sat down next to me. He was smiling, but he had tears in his eyes. "Hey, John, about the last couple of days, I am really sorry."

"Oz, I am too, I'm very, very sorry. I should never have lost my temper." We shook hands.

"I think it was inevitable, John. We both needed to clear the air. This passage has just been tough, damn tough. I didn't mean what I said yesterday."

"There was a lot of truth in what you said," I reminded him.

"The hell there was, Captain. You have sailed this boat from New York to San Francisco, or at least within 500 miles of San Francisco. That's the bottom line."

"I'll tell you what, Oz, without your patience and persistence, I think I would have gone mad long ago. Thanks for putting up with me and keeping me on course."

"John, I think we'll both be better sailors as a result of this miserable passage, and I know we'll be better friends. Now that's enough of this sentimental shit. Come on, let's eat. My powdered eggs are getting cold."

11

San Francisco—Finally!!

"It's north you may run to the rime-ringed sun, or south to the blind Horn's hate.
Or east, all the way to Mississippi Bay, or west to the Golden Gate."
The Long Trail — Rudyard Kipling

*T*HERE ARE FEW SAILORS who have endured a passage of more than 70 continuous days. Unfortunately, on May 3, it became obvious that Oz and I were going to become two of them. We were 65 days en route, still 400 miles from San Francisco, battling Force 7 head winds and bucking a stiff, contrary current. My log entry of May 3 sums up our frustration:

> *"On a day when I thought we made good progress, the noon sight tells us that we netted 53 miles; I mean 53 miles! It just makes me want to cry; we can't seem to get anywhere."*

Several days before, I had radioed Molly, who had already arrived in San Francisco, and assured her that we would be in town by May 7, 1984. However, as soon as I switched off the radio, the wind vanished.

When it returned, it blew hard and from the north. I radioed Molly again on May 4, and told her not to expect us before May 10. Molly, who was coordinating our arrival and press reception, had the thankless job of repeatedly announcing our delayed ETA.

Even though it seemed as if someone was standing on the Golden Gate Bridge and cruelly aiming a giant fan at *Gigi,* and even though we were losing 25 to 30 miles a day to the California Current, Oz and I were getting along much, much better. With the end of our protracted odyssey in sight, we were united in our desire to sail *Gigi* into San Francisco Bay. Our argument was all but forgotten; indeed, it had proved therapeutic. No amount of patience or tolerance can keep two men, cooped up in a 32-by-9-foot world for two months, from eventually exploding.

Sitting in the cockpit, bundled up to ward off the cold, Oz and I allowed ourselves an unaccustomed luxury, the luxury of dreaming. When your destination is still a long way off, it's best not to dream. I follow the old seaman's advice of: "Make yourself comfortable where you are, not dreaming about where you wish you were." However, with San Francisco just ahead, Oz and I caved in to our fantasies of what indulgences awaited us ashore and what we wanted most aboard. We devised our "10 most-wanted list":

1. Cold Beer
2. Women
3. Ice Cream
4. Oranges
5. West Wind
6. Breakfast in Bed
7. More West Wind
8. 100 Miles a Day Under Sail
9. Barbecued Steaks
10. The Morning Newspaper

On May 4, the incessant northerlies reached gale force with sustained winds of 35 knots. We held the inshore tack and beat through choppy seas. Although we pinched up as high as we could, I reckoned that we netted just 60 degrees off the wind. With her foul bottom *Gigi* made appalling and unaccustomed leeway. Still, at noon on May 5, I totalled up 78 miles — our best run in two weeks!

Sunday, May 7, I relieved Oz of his cooking duties. After much tinkering and even more cursing, I convinced the stove to throw a sporadic flame. Far from Oz's legendary Sunday brunch, I served up my usual heavy-weather fare, rubbery pancakes. Once again, I foolishly set down the bowl of batter and *Gigi* lurched over, spilling the gooey contents. The chart table received the bulk of the batter, and I was furious. Ah, but fate had finally turned our way. I pulled out the seat cushion to wipe it clean, and a beer can fell on the floor. In disbelief I shook it. It was full; it was a gift from God. Oz whooped with joy when I showed him the can of Bavaria from Chile. You must understand that we'd been out of beer for 45 days, and without spirits entirely for more than a month. I very carefully divided it, and we toasted *Gigi,* savoring every last drop.

We were closing the coast faster than we wanted, but we had no options. *Gigi* clung to a tight northeast heading, hoping to clear Point Buchon, the northwest headland of San Luis Obispo Bay. According to dead reckoning on the early morning of May 8, we were still 25 miles offshore. I scanned the horizon anyway. At first I thought my eyes were playing tricks on me, but no, it was land ho! As the sun climbed in the sky the distant outline gained definition. Although it would be five long days before we felt the actual rock, sand, and dirt beneath our feet, after 69 days of blue, rolling horizons, the greens and browns of the California coast looked magical.

We held our course until we were just a couple miles offshore and then reluctantly tacked about, heading north again. We planned to make short tacks, and I desperately hoped to pick up an inshore countercurrent. Although we were just 200 miles south of San Francisco, our food situation was critical. We had a couple of cans of tuna and tomato paste, a can of lima beans, and a few packages of noodles. For the first time I could remember, it was reassuring to have the coast close at hand.

The last five days of the voyage were the most trying of all. Strong 20- to 30-knot winds built up steep seas. Beating into steep seas was nothing new to *Gigi*. Fog, however, was. Oz and I wondered how fog could exist in 30 knots of wind. At times the fog was so thick it was impossible to see more than a few feet beyond the bow.

Fog makes celestial navigation impossible. Fortunately, the California coast is studded with powerful radio direction finding beacons. We had a hand-held Lokata unit aboard and we were able to plot reliable bearings. Yet, even if we had a good idea of where we were, there was no assurance that the many freighters plying the coastal shipping lanes knew that we were in the neighborhood. However, *Gigi* was fitted with a Combi Watchman, a radar-detection gadget that really works. When the deafening alarm would sound, we knew that a ship was nearby. The Watchman is also a direction finder and allows you to home in on an ap-

Above: Gigi *sprinting beneath the Golden Gate Bridge under spinnaker, 162 days and 16,000 miles out of New York.* **Below:** *Bill Oswald is greeted by his brother Charles in San Francisco, May 14, 1984. (Bruce Forrester photograph)*

John, Molly, and Oz toast Mayor Feinstein, who proclaimed May 14, 1984 as "Gigi Arrival Day" in San Francisco. (Bruce Forrester photograph)

proaching ship. It's eerie to slowly track the path of an invisible freighter until it's safely past. Several times we were rocked by the wakes of ships we never saw.

Slowly, we clawed our way up the coast. We had to fight for every inch, and we managed just 50 miles a day. We finally sailed out of the fog during the night of May 12. The sky was ablaze with stars, and I checked our latitude with a sight on Polaris. We were just 60 miles from San Francisco. A brilliant sunrise christened the morning of May 13, our last day at sea. I took several sun sights to confirm our position.

But the Pacific was not going to let us finish the voyage easily. We were socked in by fog just after noon, 10 miles from the Golden Gate.

"The rules of the road be damned. Oz, grab the RDF." Oz, who is a master with an RDF, homed in Point Bonita, and I steered *Gigi* recklessly through the fog. Occasionally we'd break through the fog and see the California coast off to starboard. Then the fog would close in on us again.

"Oz, there it is! The Golden Gate! There, over there!" I pointed to

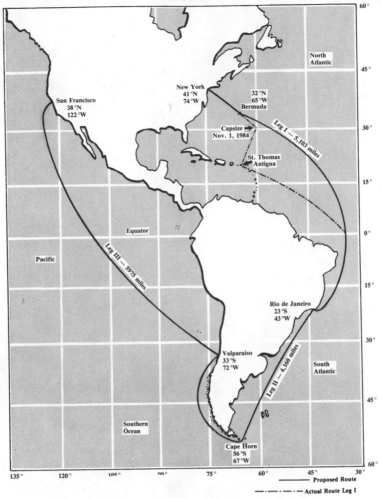

the right. The bright red Golden Gate Bridge loomed just above the fog, about five miles distant.

"We did it, we did it!" Oz shouted. We danced about, tears of joy streaming down our cheeks.

Oz took the helm and I went forward and, throwing caution to the wind, set the spinnaker. Ignoring a foul ebb tide, *Gigi* blasted through the tidal rip. At 1700, *Gigi* passed beneath the bridge, 161 sailing days and almost 16,000 miles out of New York. Our expedition was complete.

We had retraced the route of the legendary clipper ships. We had answered the wild call of the Horn by doubling the mighty Cape faster than any yacht had before. We endured a North Atlantic capsize, 120 days of head winds, and months of calms. Yet our voyage cannot be defined by statistics and records. Along the way we were enchanted, frightened, and angered by the sea and her many moods. As *Gigi* glided into her slip at Pier 39 along the wharf, I already regretted the end of the voyage. Before *Gigi*'s mooring lines were secured, I was dreaming of another voyage.